Doll Fashion Anthology Price Guide,

by A. Glenn Mandeville

featuring
BARBIE® Dolls
and other
Fashion Dolls

New Section

BARBIE® Doll Collectibles 1987-94

Published by Hobby House Press Grantsville, Maryland 21536

Dedication

This book is dedicated to the most talented person I have ever met, Dick Tahsin. His love of art, his love of life and his love for *BARBIE*® inspired this book. Enthusiasm is a great motivator! Thank you Dick, from the bottom of my heart!

Acknowledgements

Some very special people helped on this project. Sarah Eames, the "Queen of *BARBIE*®"; Bob Gantz, photographic assistance; Donna Felger, my editor; Candace Irving, former public relations director, Mattel, Inc.; Linda Collie; Marl Davidson; Franklin Lim Liao, Dick Tahsin, and Robert Tonner. The author would also like to credit the Timeless Creations division of Mattel, Inc., for the media photos of collectible *BARBIE*®.

Additional copies of this book may be purchased at $12.95 each plus $4.75 postage from
Hobby House Press, Inc.
1 Corporate Drive
Grantsville, Maryland 21536
1-800-554-1447
or from your favorite bookstore or dealer.

ISBN: 0-87588-413-X

Table of Contents

Author's Note:
Collector's demand for *BARBIE®* Dolls and *Tammy®* Dolls are robust! Prices given are subject to availability, and do fluctuate from coast to coast. The way *BARBIE®* Doll prices are rising, even if you overpay today, it may seem like a bargain tomorrow!

ALL NEW

Prices on *BARBIE®* Dolls   (Pages 182-196)
Tammy, Tressy, Judy Littlechap, et al

Coverage   (See Chapter IX)
1992 - A Most Exciting *BARBIE®* Doll Year
1993 - Collector's Influence *BARBIE®* Dolls
1994 - *BARBIE®* Doll 35th Anniversary

Introduction

The registered trademarks, the trademarks and the copyrights appearing in italics within this introduction belong to Mattel, Inc., unless otherwise noted.

If you are currently in your late 30s, you are a lucky person indeed! Over the past 28 years, starting in 1959, the world of pop culture, fashion and traditional sex roles of men and women have all gone through a radical transformation. The "baby boomers," (classified by psychologists as those now 21 to 40s),are the largest and the most spoiled group in history. Born of mothers from the Great Depression and fathers from World War II, they were the first generation in this country to grow up in a world relatively free from war and poverty. Much hope, time, money and expensive educations were put into this group of babies. Their parents hoped they would never want for anything.

All this spare time led to these children developing, in the late 1950s, their own culture, namely that of the "teenager." Up until this time children were little more than young adults, waiting to grow up into the boring world of work and obligations. The baby boomer children wanted and got more! A wonderful period in their lives developed as they reached 13, and soon an entire nation was living a life of daily "fads," created for the boom children. The world of a teenager was certainly an awesome place.

Children that today we call "pre-teens," approached this time with both joy and anxiety. Those with "bubbly" personalities, "budding" figures, pretty faces and a wealthy family certainly had little to fear. The prepubescent whose life was not so enriched had some dread. BOTH, however, needed

Revlon Dolls® is a registered trademark of Hasbro, Inc.

"lessons," as it were, to prepare for "teenhood." For some unfortunates, the world of pizza parties, soda shops and hotrods would never come. For others, these rituals needed much preparation. Suddenly little girls, especially, wanted to begin preparing for this magical time early, to better their chances of success as a teenager. (Boys were more fortunate because athletic ability was still in the passport to teen acceptance at this time, but would change later on).

This need to prepare for the future spawned an entire new generation of dolls, — the fashion doll! "Big sister" dolls with "full" figures, (consisting of huge breasts and hourglass waists) took over the place of baby and toddler dolls. The Ideal Toy Corp. was a leader in the field with the *Revlon Dolls*, which taught a young girl her first lessons in high heels and makeup. This all led, in 1959, to the epitome of the fashion doll, *Barbie*.

When first released, *Barbie* seemed the answer to many a young girl who longed to have the life-style *Barbie* seemed to thrive on. Through playing with *Barbie*, a young girl could discover the world of modeling, adventure and those mysteries such as lingerie, jewelry, hairstyles and makeup. The personal life of *Barbie...Teen-age Fashion Model* seemed threatening to only a handful of parents, as most mothers seemed eager to live through their daughters the proms, dates and dresses that the depression and war took away. *Barbie* seemed to be the answer to every prayer a pre-teen girl might have.

5

As the years rolled by, social changes came rapidly. Influences in fashion and morals came from such unlikely sources as the White House, a la Jacqueline Kennedy, and Carnaby Street in London, via Twiggy — the Mod Model. Teenagers were evolving and Barbie was changing with them. As children grew up and eased into "teendom," Barbie and her boyfriend, Ken, and other friends were right there with up-to-the-minute advice on life-styles and fashions. Mattel spent millions to develop and perfect the personality traits that Barbie possessed. By the late 1960s, the "Gidget" type of personality, that of a pretty, talented, sensitive, but down-to-earth girl, was the American dream.

When the "British Invasion" occurred after the arrival of the Beatles, Barbie again was a trend setter. As the Women's Movement took women into athletics and career moves, Barbie again helped ease the tensions of social change in her young owners.

Many young adults today, myself included, can nostalgically view a panorama of our lives through a collection of Barbie dolls and her fashions. If you were actually doing all the things Barbie was, then your view is parallel to hers, in that you can say, "I had an outfit just like that!" If fate kept you from these trends, then you can join them, still in progress within the fantasy of your own collection.

To many collectors, Barbie represents a reality and a reminder of the lives they lived. To others, it is a fantasy world they would like to have known. Whatever the reason, Barbie is like an old high school yearbook, better because she is three dimensional!

Naturally, any person or object at the top that is successful is widely imitated, in order to capitalize on the money and fame that such a position includes. Other toy companies saw a great opportunity to cash in on the teen fashion doll trend.

Some were frankly awful, merely shadows of Barbie. Others, like Ideal's Tammy, American Character's Tressy, and Remco's Judy Littlechap, took a direction all their own, and now, with our educated backward glances, we see them for the brilliant social statement they make. Often neglected by Barbie collectors, these dolls show yet another view of life in the early 1960s, a time that can never again be equaled.

Come share with me now a view of our lives, glancing backward almost three decades! Through the teenage fashion doll, our fantasies and realities mix together in a most pleasant journey. Hopefully, this book will make you smile, laugh, reminisce, and perhaps shed a tear. Most of all, it will make you remember, or meet for the very first time, a wonderful era in which to be young and alive.

Tammy® is a registered trademark of the Ideal Toy Corp.
Tressy® is a registered trademark of American Character Doll Co.
Judy Littlechap® is a registered trademark of Remco.

How to Collect Teen Fashion Dolls

As many people collect teen fashion dolls as there are dolls themselves! Collector groups and fan clubs exist all over the world. Fashion and design interest many different people from all walks of life, from those who are personally involved in the fashion world, to the most casual observer. One thing they all share, however, is their love for these little pieces of perfection.

Recently, at a *Barbie* doll convention, a gathering held once a year for dedicated fans of this American icon, I could not help but notice the diverse group of collectors: high fashion models mixed with construction workers; handicapped chatted with athletes, "macho" men laughed with ballerinas; they all shared one common interest, *Barbie*!

Barbie's fans range in age from the three-year-old receiving her first doll to a senior citizen who never heard of "The Twist." Her appeal reaches all parts of the world, where she is viewed in the ethnic guise of that particular country.

To many collectors, the fashions are the real reason they collect. Issued by the hundreds over the years, they are the gravy, the sauce, as it were, that makes the dish come alive. Mannequin-like in form, *Barbie* is to many, NOT the personality that some envision, but merely a dressmaker's figure upon which talented individuals have draped dreams over the years. To this group, the little gloves, hats and purses are like religious tokens, treasured and saved, carefully matched to each outfit.

Another group of perfectionists want, and are willing to pay for, the unopened package which contains the story of *Barbie* as much as the object sealed inside. Never has a company put so much into a box as did Mattel. The fabulous artwork and the creative packaging all add to the story of a beautiful girl's wonderful life. Yet these items bring a premium price on the collectors' circuit, because *Barbie* was meant to be played with and few early dolls and fashions survive in this condition. Those that do disappear rapidly into the ever growing numbers of private collections of those who only want mint-in-box items, driving the prices ever skyward in a spiral of supply and demand.

There are those collectors who want the glamorous gowns and sensational sheaths displayed on *Barbie* dolls where they can be viewed in three-dimensional form. Under a dome, or in a cabinet, an early *Barbie* doll, lavishly dressed, is like "stealing" a memory right out of the past and trapping it under glass for all eternity. This type of collector wants to see the garment in motion.

Thus, as there are hundreds of different *Barbie* dolls, there are just as many ways to collect. Add to this the *Barbie* family over the years, beginning with boyfriend *Ken*, and girlfriend *Midge*, and continuing with the current best friend *Whitney*, and you can see how space and money have made collectors specialize either in a particular period that they fondly remember, or a certain doll, such as just *Barbie*. Some men, angry at being denied *Ken* dolls by a sexist society, now vigorously collect *Barbie's* male counterpart and his adventuresome outfits.

Like alphabet soup, the fashion doll world is made up of many diverse people and collections. The collector soon must decide on a way to go with his/her collection!

Thus exists a unique situation to collectibles, a market within a market, generated mainly by different tastes and the overwhelming number of items available. If one were to collect "everything," and that includes licensed products from toothbrushes to bobby pins, one would literally have to turn over the entire house to one's dolls! Indeed, many collectors have done just that, bewildering friends and relatives who cannot understand why. The collector, on the other hand, smiles secretly and hopes the viewer of the collection has something in HIS/HER life that brings as much happiness.

The collector of *Barbie* and other dolls, fashions and accessories ideally should have a random sampling of boxed items because the artwork really does tell a tale of Americana as well as the dolls themselves. Then fill in the gaps with perfect outfits, with the correct accessories, displayed on the right year dolls, and the fashion story of three decades becomes complete. It is difficult at first to realize that the main piece of an outfit such as a ball gown is not where the value lies, but in the accessories. If only old vacuum cleaner bags had been saved, how many precious little necklaces and gloves would be rescued! It is these tiny cameras and travel folders, hankies and telephones, that added so much to an outfit and are so difficult to find today. The sum total of an original and complete outfit is worth so much more than the parts.

All of this only adds to the fun. Many collectors carry notebooks listing the parts and accessories they need to complete the little outfits that lovingly tell so much of our culture.

Decide on the message you want your collection to say; then figure out the best way to make it say just that! The world of the fashion dolls is an exciting place. Filled with nostalgia, romance, glamour and adventure, your collection can bring you much happiness. There are dolls and outfits available in every price range. The sheer numbers of objects manufactured make it a challange to put together an interesting collection.

If you have never thought of *Barbie*, *Tammy*, *Tressy*, et al, then read on! If you already collect, then perhaps this book will make you examine your hobby in a new light. It has been my experience that doll collectors seem just a little smarter and a little nicer than the average person. *Barbie*, of all the fashion dolls, belongs to the past and, because she is still going strong, the future is hers as well.

Some of the other dolls in our story are trapped in a time warp, destined to repeat over and over the images of the past.

Others, like Hasbro's *Jem*, and Creata's *Lace*, bring the fashion doll collector face to face with the looks of the future.

Whatever direction your collection takes, make it an outstanding display. Just like the French fashion dolls of so long ago, ages after we are all gone, a beautifully preserved doll, correctly dressed and coiffed, will tell future generations of our realities, our fantasies, our hopes and our dreams. As a fashion doll collector, we contribute much to the future. You ARE your collection. Make your dreams come true with an exciting collection of teen fashion dolls and their wardrobes!

The Care And Repair Of Teen Fashion Dolls

Some teen fashion doll collectors insist that all their dolls, clothing and accessories be never removed from box. Others enjoy the three-dimensional viewing of a mint doll dressed in a mint outfit. Still others buy played-with dolls and restore them, buying pieces of outfits, always looking for the right accessories. Many collectors, myself included, do all three! Some outfits simply look better displayed in the packaging. These outfits are usually ones that have a lot of small accessories such as trays, watermelon slices and spoons that are awkward to keep near your doll. Pieces can get lost, and so many prefer this type of outfit in the packaging.

The wonderful outfits from the couture period of the mid 1960s look fabulous on a doll, creating a three-dimensional trip backward in time! Sometimes the story on the packaging, along with the artwork is as interesting as the items inside!

The best collections, in my opinion, are made up of examples of items both in and out of the packaging. Some boxes tell the story of American fashion perfectly, and some outfits do the same. As you will discover, an outfit or doll still sealed in the package is worth twice as much as one out! For this reason, it is foolish to open a perfect old outfit. Not only that, but the collector of the future deserves to have some perfect examples left from our discoveries.

Teen fashion dolls are sturdy little dolls that basically were fashion mannequins. For that reason, many have survived with just superficial problems. You, as a collector, have to be able to see beneath the dirt and discover the treasure that is hidden! It is very rewarding to restore a *Barbie* or *Tammy* or *Tressy*, (or any doll for that matter), back to its original form.

The suggestions that follow may seem strange to you! Many may surprise you, and quite frankly, they are so easy to follow that I hate to tell "all," as it were, because we collectors are often able to buy many dolls inexpensively because the seller has not the talent nor the imagination to clean up the doll! All of these ideas are based on a lifetime of doll repair experience. The brand name products mentioned are not endorsements of that particular product or company, but simply are the ones available in my area that I have used with great success.

Tip number one is NEVER rush right home with a new purchase and start scrubbing! Live with the doll for a few days and get to know the faults and strengths before you begin any restoration project. Secondly, it is better to under restore than over restore an old doll. Some stains such as ballpoint pen ink, markers and grease just will not come out of vinyl. If you "treat" these stains too much, the color comes right out of the doll and you wind up with a worse situation. Do not buy a doll with these types of stains unless they are in an inconspicuous place.

These methods are for vinyl fashion dolls from all years and work very well. First, gather up several clean white towels, a roll of paper towels, cotton swabs, alcohol, a clean dry toothbrush, cleanser such as "Comet," a softer cleanser such as "Soft Scrub," a spray-on cleaner like "409," and liquid soap in a pump dispenser that is white like "Ivory." Additional supplies include shampoo, conditioner, plastic wrap, small orthodontic rubber bands, a metal hair pick that has a comb on the opposite end (available in dime stores), and perm wave rollers in the three smallest sizes.

IT IS MUCH EASIER TO HAVE ALL THESE ITEMS HANDY BEFORE YOU BEGIN. You can get dangerously distracted running all over the house later on, so have everything together. It is best to work on several dolls at a time, saving clothing for all at once also! You may need acrylic paints that say they can be used on vinyl such as "Flo-paque" and a small, fine quality brush for makeup touch-ups.

Let us say you have a ponytail doll that is filthy, but makeup seems intact. The legs have ground-in soil, there is a little green in her earring holes, and her hair is down and matted. BELIEVE IT OR NOT, SHE CAN BE RE-STORED TO ALMOST MINT!

Begin by washing the entire doll in the sink with liquid soap. Use a cotton swab to cleanse around facial features. Be gentle on facial makeup. Then start out with the soft cleanser and a paper towel, and try to remove the ground-in dirt on legs, arms and torso. Tougher dirt may require the regular cleanser. It will all come off! When the doll is clean, wash it again with the liquid soap and rinse well.

Dip a cotton swab in alcohol. Gently remove the head by tilting it to one side. Clean out the earring holes with the swab on both sides of the head. Replace the head.

Next, wash the ponytail in shampoo; then pour a pea-sized blob of conditioner right into the hair. Use your metal hair pick to ease knots out of the hair. When it combs smoothly with the pick, switch to the comb end and work carefully again until all the hair is smooth. You should have one long strand that stands out from the rest of the hair at the bottom. This is for the wrap around the ponytail.

Turn the doll upside down and comb all the hair up into a ponytail that sits at the crown of the head. Secure with an orthodontic rubber band (no bigger than 1/4in [.65cm] diameter). Wrap the long strand around the ponytail, and on the underside of the ponytail, lift up the rubber band with the pick and push the hair strand under it. The ponytail will now be wrapped just as it was originally. Comb the rest of the hair down straight and roll up the ends in a perm wave roller. To "set" the hair, fill a juice glass with boiling water (using caution so as not to burn yourself) and prop the doll so just the roller sits in the water! The heat will put in the set. (This can be used on an entire head, such as restoring "flips" on *Midge*®, or other dolls.) Allow the water to cool to room temperature and remove the head from the water. Let it dry overnight, remove the roller, and your ponytail is just like when the doll left the factory!

You can use the drying time to check on other things. Sometimes facial soil is heavy. Use "409" on a paper towel to remove crusts around noses and in ears. A dry toothbrush can work out this dirt for you. If your doll is missing some makeup, touch it up with the above mentioned paints, using little strokes. Just keep saying to yourself that if a factory worker could do all this, so can I! Believe me, you can.

If you want to keep the earrings in the doll, you must dip them several times in Superglue. If you do not, the earring will turn the ear area green and the doll will be ruined.

These methods work on dolls from all periods. Just be sure to be gentle on facial areas, and keep the face out of the boiling water when setting hair using this method. (Plastic wrap can act as a hair net while the doll's head is in the boiling water.)

IT IS ALWAYS BETTER TO

PRACTICE THESE METHODS ON BASKET CASE DOLLS FIRST! Buy some real pieces of junk at a flea market and see what can be done. By doing this, you can get a feel for what can be restored, and what cannot. Remember that *Barbie* and other teen fashion dolls are really display mannequins for an outfit and that some imperfections are livable to most collectors.

Mattel clothing and some garments made by other manufacturers were the finest made for any doll during the 1960s! Even more expensive clothing, made in America, could not compare to the workmanship that went into these tiny garments. Most were made of natural fibers or satins, and can be restored quite easily. AGAIN, PRACTICE ON SOME OLD CLOTHING FIRST!

Gather together several flat pans like those used for lasagna. You will also need a non-chlorine bleach such as "Clorox 2," and a regular bleach. For dry cleaning, a tightly closed jar of cleaning fluid is necessary and a sewing kit helps for repairs.

Begin by examining the garment. If repairs are needed, this is the time to reinforce seams that have pulled and repair torn hemlines. Then determine if your garment is cotton or satin (taffeta as well). For satin gowns like *Barbie's Enchanted Evening*, dry cleaning is the only safe way to restore the dress. Fill a one quart glass jar with several bottles of cleaning fluid (available at most dry cleaners) and drop in the garment. Shake the jar and that will agitate the garment. When the garment looks clean, remove it quickly. Never leave the dress in more than a couple of minutes. As you remove the garment, it will dry before your eyes as the fluid evaporates. Use this time to hand shape the garment, stuffing the body part with crumbled paper towels to hold the shape. You can even use an old doll body if you like to help shape the garment. Do not use a good doll, as the fluid may discolor the doll when wet. If light ironing is needed, use a cool iron and press on the wrong side. REMEMBER, MORE DAMAGE IS DONE BY INCORRECT IRONING THAN BY WASHING.

If your garment is cotton, or synthetic, place first in some lukewarm water to wet the outfit. Then put a cup of non-chlorine bleach into the lasagna pan. Add enough water to fill and drop in the garment. Let the dress soak for about 30 minutes. White collars can be bleached with a watered down solution of 1/2 cup bleach to 2 cups water. Use cotton swabs to get just the solution on the right places.

Finally, rinse the garment in another pan. Shake out the excess water, and again hand shape, stuffing the dress to fit the doll. Place on a clean, white towel and let dry in the sun. Check every 15 minutes or so on the drying process so you can shape the outfit as it is drying. Done correctly, you can avoid most ironing which, as mentioned, gives a shiny, overdone look to the clothes.

Dirty shoes can be scrubbed with cleanser and a toothbrush. Plastic purses and accessories can be cleaned with "409." Remember, a little time spent now will result in an object you can display with pride for years to come!

Restoring teen fashion dolls can be a rewarding way to add new dolls to your collection without spending the money for a mint doll. Teen fashion doll collecting is so much fun because, unlike other areas of doll collecting, there are so many ways to collect the same thing! Proceed carefully and confidently and you will not go wrong! Why not add a "new" old doll to your collection today!

I. Barbie® And The History Of American Fashion

Pop culture began in the late 1950s. Movies featuring teenagers and their life-styles propelled them into a longing not for adulthood, but of a time of never-never land called "teen-dom." Thus, in 1959, *Barbie...The Teen-age Fashion Model* was born, with an entensive wardrobe of fashions mirroring the current trends of style. Through the years *Barbie* would continue to reflect fashion images and values of society. Fifties' evening gowns, swinging Sixties' minis, Seventies' bell-bottoms and halter tops, to the designer dresses of the Eighties, *Barbie* has shown it all in great style!

Barbie's wardrobe was designed at Mattel by Charlotte Johnson, (later known as C.J.). Inspired by haute couture, designers such as Balenciaga, Dior, Givenchy and Balmain served as the influnce behind *Barbie's* extensive styles from her inception through 1966. Her miniature garments of fine fabric came complete with tiny zippers, buttons, luxurious linings, sparkling jewelry and above all, a name to set the mood for the outfit. Titles such as *Easter Parade, Solo in the Spotlight* and *Gay Parisienne* exemplify this technique used by the French couture designers.

The quality of *Barbie's* outfits was mesmerizing, as was the attention to detail. Since her early garments were not mass-produced, the time and care could be given to detailing a piece to

1. The epitome of early 1960s evening wear. A *Ponytail Barbie* models *Enchanted Evening* (1960), an ensemble inspired by Castillo.

2. This January 1950 *Vogue* cover clearly reflects "The Face" of the 1950s and early 1960s. Beauty was a subject of great importance and makeup helped enhance this. *Barbie's* early face mirrors this look of arched brows, side-glancing eyes and red hot lips!

VOGUE

1 9 5 0

MID-CENTURY
FASHIONS
FACES
IDEAS

ADVANC
RETAI
TRAD
EDITIO
TRAVE
HANDBOO

January 19

Price 50 Cents

3

utter perfection! The luxurious real silk full linings and hand-finished seams, hems and neatly sewn buttons gave *Barbie's* ensembles the look and quality of real haute couture. Logo signature labels were expertly sewn into each and every one!

Fashion in the 1950s was sophisticated and elegant. Women had to appear as though they had spent time making themselves perfectly groomed. "Beauty" became a subject of much importance now that wartime cosmetic shortages were over. Eyebrows were arched and darkened and lipstick gave the lips a hard line. Eye makeup varied from sultry brown to jade green; mascara was essential. Classic, yet simple hairstyles were the rule, swept up chignons worn with hats for daytime and evening, shoulder-length bobs for informal occasions. *Barbie* clearly reflected this look with her knowing arched brows, sultry side-glancing eyes, fire engine red lips and pert ponytail.

Before the mid 1960s, couture fashion took a dive into the sewing box and came up with quite a few "threads," especially for *Barbie!* The polka-dotted silk taffeta, *Gay Parisienne* (1959) was a direct offspring of Hubert

3. **The bubble dress was a mid-late 1950s fashion sensation.** *Barbie* **showed this trend in her 1959 polka-dotted** *Gay Parisienne.*

4. The late eighties saw the bubble dress once again as the fashion rage, as this fashion publication reports.

5. *Barbie's* **early fashions were inspired by haute couture designers. This 1965** *Barbie* **ensemble** *On the Avenue* **shows the Dior influence of the tailored suit accompanied by the large collared jacket.**

de Givenchy's 1956 sensation, the bubble dress. Today the bubble dress is once again the fashion rage. From Paris to the U.S., it can be seen in almost every designer's collection.

Tailored suits accompanied by jackets with large collars were very exemplary of the House of Dior's designer, Mark Bohan. *Barbie* ensembles such as *Fashion Luncheon* (1966), *Saturday Matinee* (1965) and *On The Avenue* (1965) show the Dior influence.

The great Balenciaga is clearly reflected in the outfit *Midnight Blue* (1964). Its fur collared, blue satin sleeveless cape, long white gloves and silver lamé clutch were typical accessories of Balenciaga. The 1963s *Career Girl* was yet another Balenciaga inspired ensemble. A smart, streetwise, houndstooth tweed suit, it was topped off by a matching cloche hat with rose, long black gloves and patent leather purse. This was a perfect outfit for *Barbie* to pursue her career as a fashion model.

The most popular millinery creation of all time, Balenciaga's "pillbox," was made famous by Jacqueline Kennedy, a combination of high-fashion model, movie star and royal queen. Prior to the 1960s, fashion influence had been exerted by movie stars and costume designers. *Imitation of Life* starring Lana Turner (1959), and *Back Street* starring Susan Hayward (1961) show a glittering array of "*Barbie*-like" fashions designed by Jean Louis. By the 1960s, the Hollywood star system was fading, as there were few actresses American women could emulate. Jackie Kennedy was the new clothes-conscious heroine. She spent $50,000 on her wardrobe the first 16 months after the election! Following her lead, women bared their arms to the shoulder and wore brightly colored, classic fashions. Because of Jackie,

women began wearing pillbox hats and this included *Barbie*! *Reception Line* (1965), *Theatre Date* (1963) and *White Magic* (1964) were just a few *Barbie* outfits that incorporated this millinery creation.

Barbie's most popular outerwear ensemble, *Red Flair* (1962), also came with a red velvet pillbox and flat bow. This Balenciaga-inspired coat came complete with an enormous sweep and melon sleeves.

Jackie Kennedy not only made the pillbox fashionable, but also a new bouffant coiffure known as the "bubble cut." Once again *Barbie* reflected this style, when in 1961 she was issued with not only a ponytail, but with this new style, as well!

Lurex, the metallic gold thread that swept through many fashions of the late 1950s and early 1960s, was seen on *Barbie* wearing *Evening Splendour* (1959), *Golden Elegance* (1963) and *Golden Glory* (1965).

6. *Barbie* pays homage again to the great Balenciaga wearing the chic, tweed suit *Career Girl* (1963) (topped off by a cloche hat with rose) and the ravishing velvet *Red Flair* (1962) complete with the famous "pillbox."

Women's evening wear reflected the elegance and sophistication of this period, and so did *Barbie's*! Styles which ran the gamut from the black sheath and tulle flounce of *Solo In The Spotlight* (1960), (a homage to Charles James' "tulip" gown), to the pink flowing train of *Enchanted Evening* (1960), reminiscent of Castillo.

The popularity of ball gowns was never more apparent, be they ruffled, caped or bowed. *Barbie* showed this in such ensembles as the glamorous *Debutante Ball* (1966); the red ribbon bowed *Benefit Performance* (1966); the glittering *Magnificence* (1965); and the rabbit-stoled classic, *Junior Prom* (1965).

In the mid 1960s, fashion began to focus upon teenagers. For the first time, the fashion lead came from the young, not those in the mainstream. Fashion stopped being clothing and became a value, a tool, a way of life, a kind of symbolism. Styles changed so fast that manufacturers found it difficult to produce stock fast enough. Compared with the calmer Seventies, the Sixties seemed one frenetic dash to buy the latest "look." The "look" was that of young, free, swinging, energetic — "Mod!" (a euphemism for modern). *Barbie* symbolized this new look, when in 1967 she appeared on the scene with a whole new zesty personality and wearing the garment of the decade: the miniskirt.

Mary Quant's creation of the miniskirt in 1965 was a direct result of the youth rebellion. Skirt length was a provocative statement for women, as hair length was for men. If a woman bared her knee (or more), then she was instantly identified as being "Mod." If she chose to cover it, she was assumed to be square, dull and conservative.

"The more shocking the better!"

was the fashion statement of the late 1960s. André Courregés was at the helm with such creations as the square-cut dress and flat white boots (later known as "go-go" boots). His influence was obvious in such *Barbie* outfits as *Zokko!* (1966) with its Courregés-style boots, and *Snap-Dash* (1966), a green mini trimmed in vinyl with a stylized western hat.

Paco Rabanne had shock appeal, too, with his chain-mail and plastic disc clothes, worn with huge plastic earrings. These earrings became high street fashion and *Barbie* donned them in her 1966 outfit, *Sunflower*.

The "see through look" of the late 1960s (revealing the body underneath) was interpreted in *Barbie's Jump Into Lace* (1966), a sleeveless white lace jumpsuit reminiscent of André Courregés.

The popularity of the ultra-psychedelic mini over matching tights is clearly shown in *Barbie's* outfits *Drizzle-Dash* (1967), *Togetherness* (1968), *Mini-Prints* (1968) and *Tunic 'N Tights* (1968).

Mod prints, proclaiming "Flower Power," could be seen in *Barbie* wearing *Bouncy Flouncy* (1967), *Swirly-Cue* (1968) and *Flower Wower* (1970). *Festival Fashion* was a Woodstock inspired ensemble, complete with balloon pants, fringed belt, ruffled blouse, vest and bandana head scarf. *Barbie* only needed her long hair strewn with flowers to give this hippy outfit the perfect touch!

By the end of the 1960s, the original mini had been replaced by the "micro," which climbed up the leg until it was almost thigh-high!

The fashion establishment, who was never too keen on the mini idea, fought back. Instead of the mini or the ankle-length maxi, they proposed a compromise: the midi (middle of the

calf). *Barbie's Midi Magic* (1968), *Midi Marvelous* (1968) and *Midi Mood* (1971) show her willingness to compromise!

Women either wore the mini/micro, compromised with the midi, or avoided the whole skirt length controversy with the pantsuit. *Barbie* once again mirrored this alternative, wearing such fashions as *In Stitches* (1971) and *Best Buy Fashions* #867 and #3208.

By the late 1960s, the teenagers who had drawn attention to the problems and needs of their age group were in their early twenties. As their rebellion lost its bite, the fashion mood changed.

The new mood was that of individuality, as seen in the fashions of the Seventies. Unlike the 1960s, individuality did not mean the adoption of a complete look (which was itself individual), but rather a personal style of dressing.

The uncertainty of the early 1970s led, for some people, to a return to a simpler life-style. Two social trends which affected fashion were the back to nature revival and the increasing impact of the women's movement.

7. The Balenciaga coat with enormous sweep, melon sleeves and white gloves was the inspiration for *Barbie's* most popular outerwear ensemble, *Red Flair* (1962).

8. The "original" *Career Girl* by Balenciaga.

9. Before Jacqueline Kennedy, fashion influence was exerted by movie stars and costume designers. Here Lana Turner models a "*Barbie*-like" gown designed by Jean Louis for the film *Imitation of Life* (1959).

In fashion, the shape of the body was once again emphasized by the treatment of clothes covering it, as in the Fifties, rather than by the amount of clothing that had been stripped away, as seen in the Sixties. When garments were not knitted to cling, they were cut to reveal the shape beneath. The early 1970s saw the gradual lengthening of skirts and the acceptance of pants for women, which were no longer considered unladylike. "The wider the better!" was the slacks fashion statement. One would not be caught dead in tight, straight-leg pants, quite the contrary by the end of the decade. Bell-bottoms were "it," and *Barbie* had her share of them in *Night Lighter* (1971), *Zig-Zag Bag* (1971), *Pants-Perfect Purple* (1972) and the 1970 classic, *Mood Matchers.*

The maxi coat was the early Seventies fashion sensation. *Barbie* ensembles such as *Maxi 'N Mini* (1970), *Magnificent Midi* (1971) and *Madras Mad* (1972) showed this new style. *Barbie* modeled the popular "prairie look" in such outfits as *Peasant Dressy* (1972) and *Pleasantly Peasanty* (1972).

The "gaucho" was another popular pant style in the 1970s, and *Barbie's Groovin' Gauchos* (1971) and *Gaucho Gear* (1971) mirrored the mid-calf pant craze.

Fringe was a hot detail and could be seen on everything in such fringed fashions as *Fiery Felt* (1970), *Turtle 'N Tights* (1971), *All About Plaid* (1971) and *Fringe Benefits* (1971).

The signature fabric of the Seventies was denim. Fashion designers, Calvin Klein, Gloria Vanderbilt and a host of others capitalized on this as well as *Barbie*. Denim was used from the early 1970s overall craze, *Overall Denim* (1972), to the current designer jeans trend, *Fashion Jeans Barbie* (1983).

The disco craze of the late Seventies brought sequins, spiked heels, Danskins, and three-piece white suits into the spotlight. 1977s *Superstar Barbie* and *Superstar Fashions* exuded the shimmer and shine of this beat-throbbing period.

Fashion in the 1980s saw a rebirth of the dying haute couture. Designer names like Yves Saint Laurent, Calvin Klein and Ralph Lauren became household words. Dressing up was once again sophisticated, elegant and never more carefully executed. Nolan Miller exemplified this with his glamour dressing of his "Dynasty" stars, Linda Evans and Joan Collins. Suddenly a woman could never be surrounded enough by glittering gowns and chic little suits. *Barbie* reflected this in her own Oscar de la Renta designed fashions, complete with furs, sequins and satins.

The popularity of music videos and rock stars like Madonna and

---

10. Echoes of *Barbie's Solo In The Spotlight* (1960) can be seen here in Charles James' black "tulip" gown (1950). The similarity between the two is amazing!

11

Wham brought lace, neon bright colors and wild hairstyles to the fashion world in a new way. *Barbie and The Rockers* show this "hot" new look in dressing.

The early nineties saw *Barbie* reflect the "Santa Fe" look in *Western Fun Barbie* as well as the popular primary-hued Benetton way of dressing in *Benetton Barbie*.

As we continue to move into the nineties, one can only guess what the fashion trends will be, but there is no doubt that *Barbie* will be at the forefront mirroring the newest look!

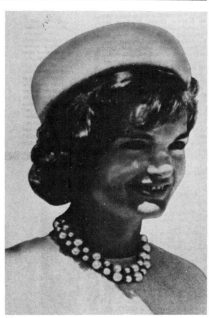

12

13

11. The "original" *Enchanted Evening* (1960) is seen here on a 1949 cover of *Vogue* magazine. This timeless creation is by Castillo.

12. In the early 1960s, Jackie Kennedy was the new clothes-conscious heroine and idealized by women everywhere. She made Balenciaga's "pillbox" famous as well as the bouffant coiffure known as the "bubble-cut."

13. During Jackie's "reign," ball gowns were very popular, be they ruffled, caped or bowed! Here *Barbie* models *Debutante Ball* (1966), one of her many ball gowns of the period.

14. The 1960s super model, Jean Shrimpton, dons the rebellious 1965 miniskirt. Skirt length was a provocative statement for women, as hair length was for men.

15. The fashion establishment, which was never too keen on the mini craze, fought back. The solution was the "midi" (middle of the calf) as seen and heard in this ad.

16. Diane Baker and "Tippi" Hedren, looking very *Midge* and *Barbie* in this 1964 Alfred Hitchcock movie, *Marnie*. (Yes, that *is* Sean Connery!) *Movie Star News* photograph.

Designers say, "What goes up must come down..."

17. During the late 1960s women wore the mini or the midi. *Barbie* mirrors this choice wearing *Rare Pair* (1970) and *Midi Magic* (1969).

18. Fashion in the early 1970s saw the acceptance of pants for women, no longer considered unladylike. Bell-bottom slacks were "it," and *Barbie* reflects this wearing 1970s *Lemon Kick!*

19. Fringe was a hot 70s detail and could be seen on everything like scarfs, sleeves, boots and, of course, hems, as seen here.

20. *Barbie* models the popular "prairie look" of the early 1970s. The back to nature revival inspired this type of dressing.

21. Designer Calvin Klein was one of the many designers who capitalized on the use of denim — the signature fabric of the 1970s. Designer jeans were a hot fashion trend of the late 70s and still are today!

22. *Fashion Jeans Barbie* was a result of the late 1970s and current designer jeans trend. The early 1980s saw society, at large, very "label" conscious as *Barbie* clearly shows with her brand boots, logo pocket and signature sweater.

23. Fashion in the 1980s saw a rebirth of the dying haute couture and clothing was once again sophisticated, elegant and never more carefully executed. *Barbie* reflects this in her own Oscar de la Renta designed fashions.

24. *Benetton Barbie* indeed does reflect the primary colors used by Benetton.

25. A rare find is this 1959 *Barbie* with original skin tones. This is the very doll that was used to make the first Mattel *Barbie* catalog for dealers. She is identified by her white irises, arched eyebrows, and the holes in her feet for her stand.

II. The Birth Of Barbie®

The late 1950s saw many cultural and social changes. "Rock and Roll," which was to liberate teenagers from the established music, was really in a downslide. Pop music had declined so much that by 1961, Lawrence Welk had a top ten hit in "Calcutta". The late 1950s saw Elvis in the army, Little Richard found God, Buddy Holly was dead, and payola scandals rocked the industry. Teenagers began to look inward to themselves for excitement and adventure. TV shows such as "American Bandstand" with host Dick Clark, and filmed live every day in Philadelphia, (THE dance capital of the US), created "stars" out of ordinary teenagers. In fact, it was the ordinary "teen" herself that was the biggest star to the younger set coming up.

Baby boom children, now around eight years old in 1959, were desperate to grow up. Role models abounded for them to follow. 1959 saw movie producer Ross Hunter bring couture to the screen with the lovely Jean Louis gowns on Lana Turner in *Imitation of Life*. More important, however, was the introduction in this movie of Sandra Dee to the American public. Before the 1960s was even half over,

26. A super prototype *Barbie*. She is made from a different material that does not fade. She has no markings, only one leg has a hole in the foot, and her make-up is totally different. She is one of about a dozen dolls that were made in Japan and sent to the United States for production approval. This doll is valued at well over $10,000!

millions of teenagers would pattern their lives after what appeared to them to be the perfect teenage girl.

All this seemed a bit overwhelming, if not downright frightening, to the eight-year-olds of 1959. Never before had it been necessary for the "ordinary" teenager to be so fashionable, so sophisticated, so ..."popular." Before, only movie stars needed to be like that. Children were fearful of not being able to live up to the expectations of teendom. A young girl of 13 suddenly found herself out of the tree house and into a crinoline, expected almost overnight to become like the teenage girls that haunted the popular television shows of the day such as "The Donna Reed Show" and "Father Knows Best."

---

27. 1959 announcement about *Barbie* **in** *Toys and Novelties,* **March 1959, issue. Billed as a "shapely teenage fashion model,"** *Barbie* **was not well received!**

Free from worry about survival like no other generation, this group of children wanted and expected their teenage years to be perfect. To accomplish this, a lot of "training" would be required. This training would have to begin early if on that magic "lucky 13" day, a young girl could make the transition.

Dolls had taken quite a turn over the past five years, as the high heel fashion doll became the staple of the doll market. What was missing from all these dolls, however, was a personality; a life-style that a girl could look up to and strive to achieve. This "personality" had to be successful without being too aggressive; pretty, but not aware of that beauty; popular, but only because she was so nice; and intelligent, but not show-offy. It was a tough package!

In 1959, Mattel was headed by a very imaginative couple, Ruth and Elliot Handler. The pair, along with a partner, Harold Matson, had founded MATTEL (MATT for Matson, EL for Elliot) in 1945. By 1946, profits were

an astonishing $30,000! The Handlers bought out Matson and went on to produce imaginative, quality toys.

The Handler's daughter, Barbara, was herself a boom child, and very much the typical little girl. She often complained to her mother that the paper dolls and fashion dolls she played with were simply not very exciting. Ruth conspired with her to make the "ultimate" fashion doll.

Things always moved fast for the Handlers and by Toy Fair, in February of 1959, they were ready with BARBIE...TEEN-AGE FASHION MODEL. The "original" doll was quite shocking to all who viewed her. Her face featured sharp, penciled-on eyebrows, and her eyes were slanted with white irises. Her very pointed features, made even more stark by her ponytailed hairstyle, seemed eerie. Also disconcerting were her large breasts which seemed a bit out of proportion to her body, which ended with long, tapered legs. Her feet were molded to fit a very high heel open toe shoe, and she came on a round, black pedestal stand that made her seem regal, but unearthly. About as far from all-American as you could get, the first *Barbie* doll, especially the brunettes, looked much like a person of mixed race.

What there WAS, however, was a wardrobe. It was this wardrobe, perfect in every detail, that sold the doll. Real satin linings in fluffy coats, couture inspired gowns and a wardrobe fit for every occasion began to shape a life-style for *Barbie* as a globe trotting fashion model that still enjoyed fun. No specific personality was established by Ruth Handler for *Barbie*. She thought the child should project her own hopes and dreams on the doll and see her own face superimposed on the blank face of *Barbie*.

28. Young girls of the late 1950s were the new baby boom teenagers such as Eleanor Donohue and Lauren Chapin of "Father Knows Best." *Movie Star News photograph.*

29. #1 Fashion booklet that came with the dolls and in all the outfits. Note the "TM" after *Barbie's* **name.** *Gay Parisienne, Roman Holiday Separates,* **and** *Easter Parade* **appeared only in this book. This was the first time** *Barbie* **was portrayed in art form.**

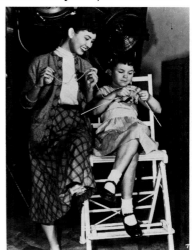

28

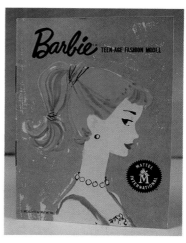

29

Undaunted, the Handlers made their smartest move. A new show, "The Mickey Mouse Club," was a Disney-produced show that featured talented children, many on the brink of "teendom." The afternoon television show was a smash hit with the boom children who viewed many of the characters, especially the older Annette Funicello, as the role model to "bridge" the gap for them between childhood and the teen years.

It is doubtful that the Handlers themselves knew the audience they were playing to when they agreed to sponsor "The Mickey Mouse Club" in 1959. The move gave them a chance to introduce *Barbie* directly to the consumer. The children loved her. Desperate to find just such a doll (like Barbara Handler was), America's children reached for the brass ring of teendom that *Barbie* offered.

By the end of 1959, dealers regretted enormously not ordering heavily on the new fashion doll, for *Barbie* had caught on where it counted ...with the child.

Refinements still had to be made. Elliot Handler said in a personal inter-

The buyers were not pleased. The doll lacked the all-American look that was popular. Larger dolls were the rage anyway, and there were plenty of other fashion dolls available for a child to play "dress-up" with.

---

30. March 1960, *Toys and Novelties* ad showed *Barbie* back for another great year. Available now were store displays and gift sets. The rich artwork on the packaging was yet to come. 31. A rare number two *Barbie* in a dressed display box. The number two doll is the same as the number one, except she has no holes in her feet. The stand is still round, but held under her arms with a black wire. The fashion is *Sweater Girl*. 32. 1960 Mix 'N' Match Gift Set. This set contained several incomplete *Barbie* outfits. The doll shown is a number five doll, already on the market by late 1960.

view with me in February 1987, that the first style *Barbie* head was made by the Japanese factory he had hired without much supervision. In an effort to cut costs, they had gone ahead with the doll. It became apparent in a short time that many parents, fresh from the Pacific theatre of World War II, did not take kindly to *Barbie's* Oriental appearance. It was just too soon. Ruth redesigned the doll, eliminating the costly holes in the feet and pronged stand, and gave *Barbie* smoother eyebrows and big blue eyes. Her makeup still remained that of a fashion model; the blood red lips and nails stood out starkly against her white skin, but this new *Barbie*, in the stores by late 1960, met her requirements.

33

Eager little girls clamored for the doll in droves. The basic doll sold for $3.00, and came with a black and white striped strapless swimsuit, gold hoop earrings, sunglasses and a round pedestal "to keep her on her feet at fashion shows." This early *Barbie* seemed down to earth enough not to be threatening, but glamorous enough to build dreams on. Just like Sandra Dee, this doll seemed to capture the soul of American teenagers without really trying.

34

The company catalog of 1959 told of Ruth Handler's philosophy about *Barbie*. "Her clothes really fit! Feminine Magic! A vertible fashion show and every girl can be the star!" Even the names of the outfits such as *Evening Splendour*, *Gay Parisienne*, *Cruise Stripe Dress* and *Roman Holiday Separates* describes the envious life-style that *Barbie* represented. Still, the little girl could CONTROL *Barbie* just by

35

33. Rare 1960 *Party Set* again with incomplete whole outfits. The doll was a number four *Barbie*. 34. Sandra Dee, THE teenager of the early 1960s. Millions wanted to be just like her! *Movie Star News photograph*. 35. By mid 1960, *Barbie's* face had been made to look more all-American. Her eyes were now blue and her eyebrows were curved. This is the number three *Barbie*, exactly as sold.

36

holding her in her hand! The future and its many threats seemed a bit less scary and more like something to look very forward to!

The success of *Barbie* in 1959 allowed Mattel, i.e. the Handlers, to rev up introductions. In what would be the first of many well timed moves, Ruth and Elliot got *Barbie* in the limelight by inventing imaginative store displays that would "catch" the eye of both parent and child right in the toy department. These store displays, a relatively new concept, acted as a permanent "salesperson," always on duty to display the items to their best advantage.

The first such display was a lovely cardboard stand that contained six plastic cylinders into which a retailer could slip a *Barbie* doll already dressed in an outfit. The background of the display used glamorous portrait shots of other *Barbie* dolls wearing the rest of the fashions available in 1960. It was a brilliant marketing strategy, and one that would propel the Handlers and Mattel into fame and fortune.

Adding to collecting history, Mattel shipped the retailer the dressed

37

36. The *Barbie* fashions were what sold the doll. Never had a doll owned such a wardrobe! Shown here is *Commuter Set*, illustrated only in the first three booklets.

37. A number three *Barbie* wears *Commuter Set*!

dolls in pink boxes with silhouettes of *Barbie* on them. The idea was once the display was outdated or an outfit discontinued, this box could be used to sell the doll. Most, if not all, retailers discarded these boxes when placing the dolls in the displays, making them a valuable collectible.

Also issued in 1960 were the first of many gift sets with names like *Party*

38. Shown only in the first *Barbie* booklet, a blonde number one models *Easter Parade* (the hat is hard to find). A number two brunette sports *Gay Parisienne* (the pocketbook is most difficult to locate). A number one blonde *Barbie* dresses in *Roman Holiday Separates* (the compact and eyeglass case are rare and difficult to obtain).

39. A close-up of a number three *Barbie* in *Easter Parade*.

Set, *Mix 'N' Match Set* and *Trousseau Set*. These did not as yet have artwork on them for the identity of *Barbie* was still that of the child, but they contained a doll surrounded by several lovely complete outfits, or in some cases, incomplete parts to mix together.

By the end of 1960, a total of three dolls would have been tried and changed. The first, with her holes in her feet for the pronged stand and her white eyes was rapidly discontinued. The second, with the same head, only no holes in the feet, still was the wrong face. A third, that had the American look with blue eyes, but still the white skin tones, lasted slightly longer.

With the introduction of the number four *Barbie* in late 1960, with her lifelike flesh tones, Mattel had made *Barbie* a household word. Scarcely

40. A number four *Barbie* with her pink flesh tones, models *Nightly Negligee*. By now, *Barbie* had that all-American look.

was a child alive that did not own or at least want a *Barbie* doll. *Barbie* was helping an entire nation of preteens grow up!

The *Barbie* era was about to begin...

III. The Early Years Of Barbie® Fashions (1959-1963)

The registered trademarks, the trademarks and the copyrights appearing in italics within this chapter belong to Mattel, Inc., unless otherwise noted.

The beginning of 1960 marked the start of a new era in America. An interesting contrast existed between the "adult" culture and teenage values. In 1960, the top three rated television shows were "Gunsmoke," "Wagon Train" and "Have Gun, Will Travel." Clearly, adults were not as interested in glamour and broken hearts as were teenagers. At the same time, the song "Teen Angel," by Mark Dinning was breaking hearts and the charts with the story of a young love that ended in tragedy. The Sandra Dee, Troy Donahue-type of love was what the young wanted. Soon, they would have it!

As mentioned in the last chapter, many collectors believe that the number four *Barbie*, with her new flesh tones, actually was the "original" *Barbie*. Now that the creation of *Barbie* was settled and she was selling briskly, she needed some sort of an identity.

Ruth Handler's son's name was Ken. In 1960, it was decided to use that name and create a boyfriend for *Barbie*. At Toy Fair, 1961, *Ken...He's a Doll* was introduced. The play on words was brilliant, as the slang "doll" was a word describing a cute teenage boy.

Ken was the perfect "boy next door" type of companion for *Barbie*.

Just looking at him, a mother knew her daughter was safe. An entire wardrobe of "activity" fashions was created for *Ken* that ranged from tennis gear to pajamas.

I cannot resist the urge to say that at *Barbie* doll conventions and doll shows in general, I am often overwhelmed by the number of men who had *Ken* dolls as a child. I did, and remember at the time loving the idea of having an idol to look up to, much the way little girls did *Barbie*. I did not then, nor do today, understand why a little boy should be denied such "friends." Thankfully, many boys are sharing love with dolls today, as boy's "companion" dolls, and *Cabbage Patch Kids* dolls are often seen in their arms. My entire love of dolls today as an adult is based on my wonderful shared experiences with my *Ken* doll!

---

41. The exciting new "bubble cut," on *Barbie*, wearing *Solo in the Spotlight*! This was one of *Barbie's* most famous outfits!

Cabbage Patch Kids® is a registered trademark of Coleco Industries, Inc.,

By 1961, the world of *Barbie* was moving ahead. A popular television show that year was "Hawaiian Eye," and featured a lovely young *Barbie*-type, Connie Stevens, as Cricket Blake. Cricket still had her long blonde pony-tail, but the entire front of her hair had been layered into a new style, the bubble cut. Teens everywhere began copying her hairstyle, and many took the plunge and removed the long back. Mattel responded by issuing *Barbie* in the new *Bubble Cut* version. The lips were still red and really nothing was different except the hairstyle. Starting with the ponytail dolls this year, a new material, Saran, was used for the entire ponytail head including the bangs. This firmer banged doll is considered

42

43

42. America's dream couple. *Ken, He's a Doll*, and *Barbie, Teen-age Fashion Model Doll*.

43. 1961 saw the addition of redheads to the line. Officially called "Titian," the color was that of the real life *Barbie*, Barbara Handler. These dolls were made at the ratio of 1 to 100 blondes, and are today quite rare.

44. The new 1961 *Bubble Cut Barbie* and the ponytail *Barbie* of that year. The dolls were identical except for the hairstyle.

the number five *Barbie*. It is at this point that the numbering stops. After this, so many changes in lip color and hairstyling existed that numbering would be impossible. Also new in 1961 was the addition of redheads to the line. Ruth Handler had a special place for red or "titian" haired dolls, for the real life *Barbie* had this color hair!

In 1962, Ken became a sturdier doll. The 1961 version had a type of molded head with "flocked-on" hair. It looked wonderful, (just like a crew cut), but when it got wet, the flocking came right off.

This new 1962 Ken had hair molded in the new "butch" cut. This style left a longer strip of hair along the front of the head that was pushed up every morning with a "butch" wax stick! Girls were not alone in their obsession with hair!

Fashion was changing and so was makeup. Teen girls now were tiring of the blood red lips popular in the late 1950s. Paler lips and softer eye makeup was the new "in" thing. *Barbie* reflected this in 1962 with lips in varying shades.

Many long-time buyers of *Barbie* remember, like I do, of seeing a friend have a particular doll, and then going to the store to find it! There were endless variations, just like there are today with *Cabbage Patch Kids*. My young experience was to sit there and pull down doll after doll, lifting the lid of the box, until the store employees finally politely asked me to leave! In fact, a close friend of mine had a doll that was an ordinary blonde bubble, but with white lips, that I did not see again for 25 years, when I finally found one at a local show! Many collectors are not aware of just how mass-manufactured and how different these dolls were. By 1961, over six million *Barbie* dolls a year were pro-

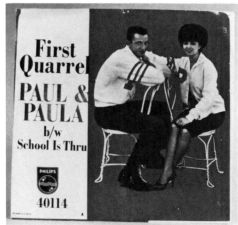

45

46

45. 1961 bubble-cut *Barbie* and *Ken's* resemblance to real people is astonishing, as shown in this record cover by Paul and Paula.

46. **A number five ponytail *Barbie* and *Ken* model *Registered Nurse* and *Dr. Ken*. Of course, *Barbie* had to be the nurse. It would be 20 years before *Barbie* would get a doctor's uniform and diploma!**

47. Troy Donahue seems to exemplify the *Ken* look! In this photograph he is even wearing *Ken's* outfit, *Time for Tennis!* *Movie Star News* photograph.

48. The lovely Diane Baker, shown in this 1961 publicity photograph, was the epitome of *Bubble Cut Barbie!* She would go on to change her hairstyle exactly to what *Barbie* would wear in 1964! *Movie Star News* photograph.

47

48

49. Very collectible items from this period are the *Dressed Box Dolls*. The boxes were "banded" to identify them. Shown are *Tennis Anyone* on *Barbie* and *Time for Tennis* on *Ken*.

49

50. The adventures of *Barbie* and *Ken* were so exciting to youngsters that gradually distinct personalities evolved for *Barbie*. Dell comics published an entire series of comics that depicted their lives in teenage splendor!

50

duced. This is the reason why out-of-box dolls from this period are not worth much. Every little girl alive had one or more *Barbie* dolls and many have survived in excellent condition.

By 1963, dazzling artwork on the *Barbie* packaging told the story of a beautiful girl's wonderful life almost as well as the dolls themselves.

Ruth Handler was being urged more and more to establish a personality for *Barbie*, something that she rebelled against.

As a compromise, the line was expanded. A new doll, *Fashion Queen Barbie*, was issued that consisted of a molded head and three very high style wigs. There was a redhead "flip" inspired by Shelley Fabares of "The Donna Reed Show," a white or platinum "bubble on bubble," and a Cleopatra style of a brunette "page boy." There was still lots of choice for a little girl. *Barbie* could be a projection of the child's identity as Ruth Handler

wanted, or have her own personality. It was hard for *Barbie* not to have a personality when she had a boyfriend, and now a girlfriend, *Midge*!

Midge was the doll that, in my opinion, cemented the idea of a personality for *Barbie*. *Midge* was the perfect best friend. Not envious, but supportive, she was very willing to play a secondary role in *Barbie's* adventures. *Midge* was the type of girl that knew she could not be "Queen of the Prom," but was thrilled to get close to it through her association with *Barbie*.

Random House published a series of novels about *Barbie, Ken* and *Midge* that told of their lives in Willows, Wisconsin, a fictional town that could be "Anywhere USA." *Barbie* and the

51. A studious *Barbie* and her dog study hard for finals. She is wearing *Ken's* shirt. The shoes and socks are from 1980s dolls!

52. Mint in box vintage dolls. Number one "flocked hair" *Ken*, the new 1962 *Bubble Cut Barbie* in red swimsuit, a "swirl' ponytail *Barbie*, and the second issue of *Ken* with molded hair. Dolls in this condition are worth more than double dolls out of the box.

53. During this period, the Suzy Goose Company made gorgeous furniture for *Barbie*. Shown is a number four *Barbie* in *Nighty Negligee* and *Midge* in *Sweet Dreams*.

54. The accessories for the clothing are the difficult part to locate today. Shown is *Candy Striper Volunteer* for *Barbie* and *Campus Hero* for *Ken*. The little spoons, boxes of tissues and varsity letters are what drive collectors crazy when trying to complete an outfit!

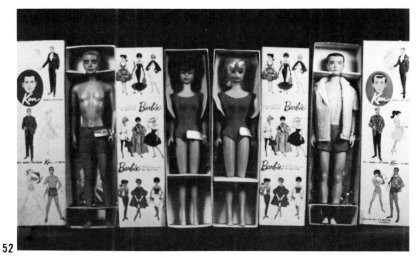

52

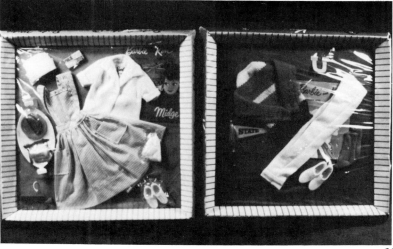

53

54

55. *Playthings Magazine* ad for March 1963, saw the addition of *Fashion Queen Barbie* and wigs to the line. The store display shown was available to the retailer. Mattel was one of the first companies to use this method of marketing.

gang attended Willows High; all the beautiful things that happened to *Barbie* just DID. She, like Bill Woggon's *Katy Keene*, was a beautiful, shy, down-to-earth girl that no one could resent.

The life of *Barbie* was an enviable one. A set called *Barbie Baby Sits* was created to concentrate on the "average girl" aspects of *Barbie's* personality. Her link to the world of high fashion was lessening. Most, if not all, of the Mattel licensed products from the period reflect the idea that *Barbie* and *Ken* were just average teenagers that were born leaders. This was an ideal that the television shows of the day aspired to greatly. Even brother teams like Wally and Beaver on "Leave it to Beaver" were children you could be

proud of. There was a satisfaction often missing today in making the honor roll, being a crossing guard, and serving as lunchroom monitor. If, through all this you could be pretty, popular and well-groomed, well, the brass ring was yours. At least this was the dream that was told to the baby boomers. Later on this dream, for some, would turn into a nightmare, especially for some women who would realize that Cinderella was often just a prisoner in a castle. But for now, being "perfect," according to the standards of the day, was a goal all its own.

The *Barbie* fashions of this and the couture period were the best ever made. Zippers that really zipped, tiny charm bracelets and real silk linings gave the clothing a tailored look that

56

56. Naturally a fashion model had to have a place to model her fashions. This *Fashion Shop* was a clever cardboard shop for *Barbie.* *Midge* waits at the model's entrance in *After Five.* *Ken* is the escort in *Country Clubin'* and *Barbie* models *Career Girl.*

57. Inside the *Fashion Shop,* *Midge* models *Senior Prom* and *Barbie* wears *Sophisticated Lady.*

57

58. Irwin Plastics in New York had the license for many clever *Barbie* accessories. Shown are *Barbie* in *Resort Set* going sailing with *Ken* in *The Yachtsman!*

59. *Barbie* got a little sister, *Skipper*®, in 1964. The "family" concept was expanding, as was the imaginative themes for outfits such as these masquerade costumes.

---

today is viewed as magical. The tiny garments are so perfectly made that if enlarged, they would suffice even the fussiest of dressers. Adding to the appeal of every *Barbie* outfit was a label identifying it as a genuine *Barbie* fashion, and obviously of superior quality. Tiny velvet lined purses, white tricot gloves and the perfect footwear for each ensemble added to the mystique of these outfits. Other companies tried to copy Mattel's style. In fact, *Barbie* was and is the most imitated fashion doll in history. The truth is that nothing ever came close and probably never will in terms of fashion quality and theme selection.

The outfits were assigned a stock number, in the early period a 900 series number. This was not to aid the child or the collector, but for the merchant to identify and inventory his stock. For this reason they have been omitted from the text and illustrations as often they are not continuous and can be confusing.

There is one thing for certain. By 1964, *Barbie* was the dominating force in the toy industry. In order to retain that title, many revisions would have to take place. Teenagers were on a roller coaster ride of fads and fancies. Could *Barbie* remain "Queen of the Prom" in the toy world?

We already know the answer to that astounding question. *Barbie* did go on to the couture period, a period inspired by a great lady, Jacqueline Kennedy. Just ahead for *Barbie* was college and a more "mature" way of dressing. The boom children were growing up and so was *Barbie!*

60. Spectacular gift sets were available during the early 1960s, such as this *On Parade* set. It is very rare to find these sets unopened today. They are valued at well over $500 each when in this condition.

61. Available for *Barbie* were many *Paks*, or cheaper separate pieces for outfits. This rare set called *Mix 'N' Match* shows *Barbie* and her many *Pak* fashions.

62. *Barbie* shows her versatility in this *Round the Clock Gift Set*. Outfits are *Career Girl, Fancy Free* and *Senior Prom* with the addition of a fur stole!

63. *Barbie* and *Ken* wearing *Open Road* and *Rally Day*, go for a spin in Irwin Plastic's *Ken's Hot Rod!*

64. *Barbie* in *Enchanted Evening*, one of the all-time favorite outfits, escorted by *Ken* in *Tuxedo*. Playing the rare Suzy Goose Piano is *Allan, Ken's Buddy* wearing *Best Man*.

65. *Skipper* got a new friend, *Skooter*, in 1965, but she looks so good in *Red Sensation*, I had to use her! *Fashion Queen Barbie* models *Sheath Sensation*.

66. Teenage life is depicted with uncanny reality in *Barbie* outfits and accessories. Here in the *Campus Sweet Shoppe, Barbie* wears *Friday Night Date, Ken* sports *Dreamboat, Allan* is wearing *Play Ball* and *Midge* rests in *Pak* separates.

67. The richness of the lavish fashions is seen here in *Midge* wearing *It's Cold Outside*, in the rare red version, *Barbie* shows off *Red Flair* (the longest running outfit of the early period) and *Skipper* looks lovely in *Dress Coat*.

68. Millions of children acted out teenage life with their dolls. The clever themes of the fashions allowed realistic play. Shown are *Ken* in *Fun on Ice*, *Barbie* in *Ice Breaker* and *Skipper* in *Skating Fun*.

69. The winter fun possibilities were endless for *Barbie* and the gang. *Barbie* is wearing *Ski Queen*, *Ken* in *Ski Champion*, *Skipper* is in *Sleddin' Fun* and *Midge* models *Winter Holiday*.

47

70

71

72

70. Whitman made lovely paper dolls of *Barbie* and *Midge* during the early years. The personality of the two girls can be readily seen. These, uncut, are worth $25 each.

71. Afraid to make *Barbie* too sophisticated, Mattel toned down her high fashion image. *Barbie* was a down-to-earth girl who baby sat, as in *Barbie Baby-Sits*, and had a pet dog, shown in *Dog & Duds*.

72. Drive-ins were popular with teens in the early 1960s. Shown in Irwin Plastics *Barbie's Car* are *Barbie* in *Movie Date*, *Ken*, *Midge* and *Allan* wear *Pak* fashions. The backdrop is a lovely scene from *Barbie Goes to College*.

73

74

73. The easygoing teenage life depicted in *Ken* wearing *Sailor*, *Barbie* in *Garden Party*, *Midge* in *Let's Dance* and *Allan* in *Army Air Force*. It was still patriotic to depict sterotypical roles for teens.

74. Frivolous fun for *Barbie* and *Midge* in *Suburban Shopper* in blue and *Busy Morning* in red! The tiny dial phones and decorated purses are hard-to-find accessories today.

75. Serious careers were depicted for *Barbie* and *Ken* such as *Barbie* in *American Airlines Stewardess* and *Ken's American Airlines Pilot*. Teenagers were growing up and so was *Barbie!*

75

IV.
The Couture Period
(1964-1966)

As mentioned previously, the baby boomers were growing up. Many, by 1964, were graduating from high school, and were on their way to college. Never had so many from one generation gone on for higher education. A "liberal arts" degree (bascially meaning you were versed somewhat in ALL areas), was the "American Dream." Later, only those with highly specialized skills would be employable, but for now, just having a college degree would be enough. Many high schools boasted that up to 90% of their graduates went on to college, and often this became the focal point of education.

The next generation coming up was faced with a more mature role model. The James Dean and Natalie Wood-type of the late 1950s teen had learned that reckless fun was too costly. The Sandra Dee, Troy Donahue crowd were getting married! Younger preteens found themselves looking to older women such as America's First Lady, Jacqueline Kennedy, and later, Lady-bird Johnson. Even the top rated television show of 1964, "Bewitched," starred an older, married woman, Elizabeth Montgomery.

If one had to name an influence on fashion for the beginning of the decade, it would have to be Jacqueline Kennedy. Born into aristocracy, she was the closest to a queen this country ever had. Columnists delighted in listing her ensembles on the society pages; designers were glad to be designing for women instead of teenagers.

In 1964, Mattel made the decision to allow *Barbie* to grow up. Graduation outfits were available, and a set, *Barbie Goes to College*, with a dorm room for *Barbie* and *Midge* replaced the *Dream House* of *Barbie's* high school years.

The women's movement was just getting under way. Along the road to the "American Dream," women were realizing that they, too, had more to offer society than dirty diapers. As women attended colleges and universities in record numbers, they became aware of just how they had been shortchanged by society, as far back in this country as the Constitution, which did not even allow them basic human rights such as voting. They wanted and got more. Change was the password of this period.

---

76. This rare *Color Magic Face* side-part *Barbie* models Sears exclusive mink coat, 1964-1965.

77. The back of the *Fashion Queen Barbie* box told the beautiful story of a fashion model's life. By now, the identity of *Barbie* was well established.

78. A lavish gift set featuring *Fashion Queen Barbie, Ken* and their trousseau was on the market during this period. Unbelievably rare today, it brings, unopened, over $700!

79. *The Wedding Party Gift Set* allowed for fantasy play about the wedding of *Barbie* and *Ken*. Officially, they have never been married to this day!

80. Friends of *Barbie* and *Ken*, as these shown in perfect as new condition, expanded play possibilities and taught children about relationships among friends. From left, *Ricky*, *Midge*, *Allan* and *Skooter*.

81. *Barbie* and *Ken* graduated from high school in 1964 and, of course, went on to State "U."

82. In 1964, Mattel issued *Miss Barbie*. She was the only doll issued with a hard plastic head and sleep eyes. Goulish in appearance, she was rapidly discontinued, leaving an outstanding, but bizarre collectible.

83. *Barbie* was the perfect college student. Naturally, her modeling experience led to acting. In her *Little Theatre*, she, *Ken* and *Midge* act out the timeless drama of *Cinderella*.

Mattel felt that the next group of youngsters would like to see *Barbie* as a career woman. Her relationship with her high school sweetheart, *Ken* did not lead to marriage and babies, (much to the concern of many moralists of the day), but to various "careers." During this period *Barbie* became an art critic, as well as an artist, a student teacher, a fashion editor, an entertainer, an actress in little theatre, a world traveler, and still retained her interest in modeling!

Barbie excelled at college just as she did in high school. As a sorority sister, homecoming queen and cheerleader, she was second to none!

Little girls had tamed down a bit from their desire to grow up; to satisfy this need to play with an alter ego, Mattel issued *Skipper*. She, along with *Ken*, would remain at *Barbie's* side for the next 28 years. Billed as *Barbie's Little Sister*, *Skipper* had matching "junior-edition" size fashions that corresponded to *Barbie's*. The same care and workmanship went into *Skipper* as did *Barbie*. Her clothing and her life-style was spelled out to the buyer on the wonderfully designed packaging of the period. Like *Midge*, *Skipper* was willing to play a supportive role, but you knew by the twinkle in her eye that some day she would come close herself to being like *Barbie*.

Trapped in pertpetual puberty, *Skipper* throughout the years has remained loyal to all of *Barbie's* dreams and ideas, never forsaking them for her own.

Experimentation abounded at Mattel in 1964. *Midge* got a new boyfriend in *Allan*. Billed as *Ken's Buddy*, it was a natural foursome. *Allan* was just like *Midge* in that he was loyal to *Ken*, and acknowledged that there was nothing wrong in being either the leader or the follower, if one

84

85

84. Foreign travel as an exchange student was necessary for all college bound boom children. Here *Midge* and *Allan* visit Holland, while *Barbie* and *Ken* return from Mexico. Other *Travel Outfits* included a pair of Swiss outfits, a pair of Hawaiian togs and a kimono for *Barbie*.

85. The big news of 1965 was "Lifelike Bendable Legs." The dolls were all updated to a "preppie" image that would last only two years. Notice the shy look for *Ken* this year!

was content in the role. This was a valuable lesson and one that is often forgotten today. Without Indians, there could be no chiefs! 1980s parents tend to push all of their children into leadership, when many would make wonderful, happy followers. The end result is often disastrous. *Ken*, and his relationship with *Allan*, taught many little girls (and boys) lessons of life they could not have learned elsewhere.

86. A new hairstyle, nicknamed "The American Girl," arrived with a bang. Featuring one length sides and back ("blunt" cut), and flirty bangs, it would later resurface in 1981 as Linda Evans' signature hairstyle! Here movie actress Yvonne Craig, ("Batgirl") shows off her new "do." *Movie Star News photograph.*

87. *Jack and Jill* magazine often ran ads for *Barbie* dolls. Note the "American Girl" hairdo on the mother in this 1965 ad.

88. The couture period at its high fashion best shown here in *Gold 'N Glamour* (1965), *On the Avenue* (1965) and *Saturday Matinee* (1965).

Many other doll companies were using innovative ideas that were spawned of the post war prosperity. Mattel, eager to retain *Barbie's* crown, issued a *Miss Barbie*, which had a sleep eye feature and hard plastic head. If ever a doll had no personality, this was it! Bland, and almost goulish, it rapidly faded from view, but left a valuable collectible.

1965 was a big year for *Barbie*. This year she and her friends got "bendable legs." This feature was wonderful, and allowed the dolls to pose realistically. The technology was very advanced, for a knee joint was inside the leg, and from the outside could not be seen. Billed as "lifelike," it certainly gave new dimension to the dolls.

Also new in 1965 was a hairstyle for *Barbie* called the "American Girl." Basically a chin length blunt cut with bangs, it was more youthful than the teased bubble cuts. This style also

89. There is nothing like double dating and *Barbie, Ken, Midge,* and *Allan* do just that! A stunning blonde side-part *Barbie* models *Fraternity Dance* (1965), *Ken* dons *Tuxedo,* *Allan* sports *Best Man,* and *Midge* wears *Holiday Dance* (1965).

90. **Different colors of** *Barbie's Sweater Girl,* **available since 1959, appeared. These are in pink and navy blue.**

91. Back from the 1966 Spring Fashion Show, *Bendable Leg Barbie* models her new purchases; left, *Reception Line* and right, *Fashion Luncheon*.

92. Winning awards was part of college life! Here *Barbie* shows off her oil painting skills in *Modern Art* (1965) and *Poodle Parade* (1965). These outfits, made only for one year, and having many accessories, are very difficult to locate complete. (Years are given for these outfits to help the collector see the limited availability.)

93. *Bendable Leg Barbie* and *Midge* take the scene in style. *Midge* wears *International Fair* (1966) and *Barbie* sports *Matinee Fashion* (1965).

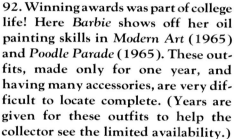

94. The concept of matching outfits for *Barbie* and *Skipper* was continued throughout the period. Here our girls are shipbound in nautical inspired attire. *Barbie* wears *Aboard Ship* (1965) and *Skipper* poses coyly in *Ship Ahoy* (1965).

95. *Midge* and *Allan* pose for a candid snapshot. *Midge* wears *Beau Time* and *Allan* sports *Rovin' Reporter*.

96. 1966 saw the introduction of *Color Magic Barbie.* Her hair could change colors with an applied solution that could also change the color of her special outfits. Although mass marketed, she is most difficult to locate today.

96A. The 1967 version of *Color Magic Barbie* with its new, unique cardboard packaging. This version is extremely rare and valued at well over $1,000!

97. *Ken* and *Barbie* were BOTH astronauts in 1965, boosting the fledgling woman's movement. Twenty-two years later, *Barbie* would again be a space explorer!

98. Couture period outfits were beautifully made and highly accessorized. Shown are *Barbie's Dancing Doll* (1965) and *Skipper's Me 'N My Doll* (1965). Contained in this set is a tiny *Barbie* doll for *Skipper* to play with!

99. By the mid 1960s, vinyl houses had replaced the cardboard structures of the early period. This house is very unusual and features a typical period living room.

100. The lavish artwork on all *Barbie* accessories told the lifestyle of *Barbie* beautifully. Here *Barbie* is dressed in *Riding in the Park* (1966) and poses with horse *Prancer*.

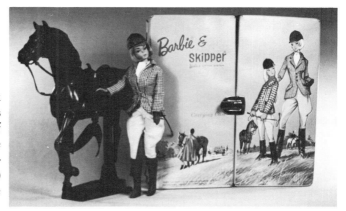

101. A stunning red-lipped *Bendable Leg Barbie* is ready to go on stage in the rare *Benefit Performance* (1966).

102. The down-to-earth qualities of Barbie are featured in these school outfits. Ken wears *College Student*, *Barbie* is busy as a *Student Teacher* and *Skipper* is the perfect *School Girl*!

heralded the beginnings of long, straight hair that would dominate fashion for the next ten years.

All the "bendable leg" dolls were mass manufactured but today, for some reason, are difficult to locate in original packaging.

Both *Barbie* and *Midge* were available as separate molded heads in a *Color and Curl Set* that featured red and blonde wigs that could be colored and set. Actually, this was the first type of wig or hair on *Barbie* that actually could be "set." The other fibers used had the curl put in at the factory by a heat method and could not be changed. The styling possibilities were endless, and the set worked even better than advertised!

1966 saw this curlable, colorable hair rooted right into the head in *Color Magic Barbie*. This doll added the versatility of real hair play, absent since *Barbie's* birth. The doll is a delight and somewhat difficult to find today in good condition, due to the many "beauty" sessions she undoubtedly had to endure.

Also in 1966 *Skipper* got a new friend, *Skooter*. 1965 saw a little boy, *Ricky*, join the group, and *Skooter* completed the picture. Both had the "follower" type of personality that all of *Barbie's* friends had and would have until *Barbie's Modern Cousin, Francie* arrived later in the year!

Francie is my favorite of all the *Barbie* family dolls, and it is a great temptation to devote an entire chapter to her. The mid 1960s saw the arrival of many British rock stars. The Beatles, already a household word, were taking teens out of the matronly look just

103. Ball gowns abounded during the mid-1960s. A rare ash blonde, side-part *Barbie* models *Debutante Ball* (1966) while her escort, *Ken*, wears *Summer Job*.

recently made popular and into wild, outlandish styles.

Mattel, already quaking with having put *Barbie* into an older, more sophisticated look, was stumped! Would this Mod thing last? What did teenagers want? Board meetings were held and it was decided that for at least another year *Barbie* would be left untouched. To satisfy the Mod type of child, *Francie* would be introduced.

Loosely based on the character Francie Lawrence (Gidget), *Francie* was the epitome of the character played by Sandra Dee in movies and Sally Field on television. *Francie* was smaller than *Barbie*, but her fashions had a "Carnaby Street," London flair. She also featured a new innovation, rooted eyelashes! *Francie* would be so popular that next year *Barbie* would be redesigned to look more youthful, more energetic...more like *Francie*! For the first time *Barbie* was to be a follower. The only saving grace was in the stories about *Barbie* and *Francie* in the *Barbie Magazine* (the official Fan Club publication). *Barbie* was older, and therefore wiser. It still was a year before the Beatles would say, "Never trust anyone over thirty!"

The "family" concept of *Barbie's* world was becoming very enticing. Other dolls such as Remco's *Littlechap Family* and Ideal's *Tammy* and her family necessitated the move to expand the original *Barbie* concept.

1966 also saw the introduction of *Tutti, Barbie and Skipper's Little Sister*, and her twin brother, *Todd*. Smaller than *Skipper*, these little dolls were a

104. From formals to hostess wear, *Barbie* had it all. Here a *Midnight Color Magic Barbie* serves up tea in *Barbie's Hostess Set*. The ensemble was the red version of *Invitation to Tea* (1965).

105. The end of the couture period saw the last of "traditional" fashions for over a decade. *Barbie* and *Ken* play at marriage in 1966 with *Here Comes the Bride* and *Here Comes the Groom*. These outfits, like the life-style they depict, are rare today! Just ahead was the British Invasion and MOD!

106. *Barbie* takes the loving cup as Prom Queen in 1964 dressed in *Campus Sweetheart* (1964-65). Her moment of triumph is richly illustrated on this board game from the period.

105

107. More fabulous couture gowns! These rare outfits are *Formal Occasion* (1967), *Midnight Blue* (1964) on a rare white lip *Barbie* (remember those AWFUL lipstick colors?) and *Evening Enchantment* (1967).

108. The popularity of "Lurex" gold thread used in period clothing, reflected in couture *Barbie* clothing. Left is *Holiday Dance* (1965), middle is *Golden Glory* (1965), and on the right, *Evening Gala* (1966).

delightful addition to the *Barbie* family. Together, *Barbie, Ken, Midge, Allan, Skipper, Skooter, Ricky, Francie, Tutti* and *Todd* all made up the "American Dream Family" and their friends. The couture period, like President Kennedy's life, was over almost before it began.

Next year, an entire new look for *Barbie*!

109. *Barbie* bids adieu as she takes flight in the rare *Pan American Airways Stewardess* from 1966. She will return from her trip with an entirely NEW look the next year!

V.
The Mod Scene
(1967-1971)

1967 was really an important year in pop culture. The "British Invasion" of rock music and clothing styles from England was starting to make even the most conservative teenagers turn more "Mod." Magazines such as *Seventeen*, *Glamour* and even *Vogue* were leaning more toward "young" fashions instead of the classic, but matronly Jacqueline Kennedy type of dress. "The Motown Sound," using black groups like "The Supremes" were gaining air time in white clubs and radio stations. Cultures were blending as youth forgot about tradition.

It must be pointed out that these influences were NOT just associated with the lower and middle classes. College students from the finest universities also had become "Mod." It was strictly fashion and music FUN!

Barbie, by the start of this period, had really become very high fashion, with the pillbox hat and suit look. With the popularity of *Francie*, and her "Mod" wardrobe, Mattel thought it safe to loosen up *Barbie* and go with the youth movement. Afraid to resurrect the controversy *Barbie* caused in 1959, Mattel moved cautiously.

The real support for *Barbie* being a bit more modern came from the boom children themselves. Annette Funicello, once the "Now It's Time to Say Goodbye" sweetheart of 12 on the

"Mickey Mouse Club," had grown up into a busty, sexy young lady! Looking a lot like *Barbie* herself, she still retained innocence in her *Beach Party* movies, as did Sandra Dee earlier in *Gidget*.

Mattel wasted no time. At Toy Fair, 1967, a NEW *Barbie* was introduced. The same size and shape, the big change was her face. Made from a new mold, it mirrored the "growing up young" look that was popular. Available in such hair shades as "Chocolate Bon-Bon" and "Go Go Co-Co," the doll featured the new long straight hair with bangs ("fringe" if you were Mod) and rooted eyelashes! A new advance, a twist and turn waist, made this *Barbie* more posable than ever before.

In May, a huge trade-in program was launched, where a child could bring in an old doll, and for $1.50, receive a brand new one. The dolls were traded in by the millions, with the old dolls given to charity. (This accounts for the scarcity of the number one and number two dolls.) Also available was a standard version of the

---

110. The ultimate Mod outfit, *Zokko*, is *Barbie's* choice in a Carnaby Street polka dot room! *Barbie* now has a younger, more youthful face, and long, swingin' straight hair.

111. A relaxing moment for a 1967 *Twist 'N Turn Barbie* in *Mini-Prints* never shown in any fashion booklet!

112. Even the 1967 paper dolls showed that "*Barbie* Has a New Look!"

113. The 1967 trade-in offer led to the turning in of millions of older dolls. For $1.50 a child could get a new doll in exchange for an old doll.

114. *Barbie Talk* advertisement for the "trade-in" dolls.

115. *Twiggy*, London's top fashion model, joined the Mattel doll family in 1967. She was able to wear all of *Francie's* MOD fashions, as illustrated here wearing *Style Setters*, never shown in any fashion booklet! The *Twiggy* outfit is *Twiggy-Do's*.

116. The Mod influence is shown in *Barbie's Trail-Blazer* outfit from 1967, *Francie's Merry-Go-Rounders* from 1969 and *Skipper's Pink Princess*, 1970.

117. *Barbie's MODern Cousin, Francie* was a major influence on fashion trends. A 1966 straight leg *Francie* is shown modeling 1969 *Land Ho!*

118. 1967 saw *Francie* get a friend, *Casey*. She could wear all the groovy Mod fashions such as *The Yellow Bit* from 1969.

---

doll with straight non-bendy legs and no eyelashes.

Perhaps the biggest news of 1967 was the introduction of a black version of *Francie*. Identical to the white doll, she was a complete failure. Blacks still longed to buy into the American dream through fantasy. *Barbie* and her family were white and espoused the ideal that EVERYONE, black and white ascribed to. Years later blacks would want the American dream of their own and ethnic dolls would be popular. It was just too soon in 1967.

Barbie's world got many new

"friends" that year. *Tutti, Barbie's Little Sister*, appeared in several new play sets that featured well done accessories like swings and stoves. She also got a new playmate, *Chris*. Available in blonde and brunette, *Chris* and *Todd* (*Tutti's* brother) were the junior set.

The favorite new doll of the year was that of *Twiggy*, London's top fashion model. Volumes could be written on the psychology of a scrawny kid with a cockney accent that changed the entire world! *Twiggy*, in doll form, was stunning, with a *Francie*-sized body so they could share Mod fashions.

119. A 1968 *Talking Barbie* models 1969s *Country Capers,* while a 1967 *Twist 'n Turn Barbie* shows off *Fashion Shiner,* of 1967. The matching paper dolls were an art into themselves.

120. The heroes of the baby boomers themselves were growing up! Shelly Fabares, who led many a child into teenage life on "The Donna Reed Show," sported the same hairstyle as *Barbie* in 1967! *Movie Star News photograph.*

121. Even Annette Funicello from the "Mickey Mouse Club" was growing up! Her "Beach Party" type movies were taking "Gidget" another step forward! *Movie Star News photograph.*

Francie, Casey and *Twiggy,* (*Casey* was another American friend of *Francie,* who had short hair in a "Sasson" cut, and wore one dangling triangular gold earring!) went everywhere together. This, again, was fulfilling Ruth Handler's original concept that the choices were many for a child who selected *Barbie* and her world to play with. If the child wanted to grow up glamourous, there was *Barbie.* If she wanted to be the new type of "Mod Teen," there was *Francie;* if the little girl wanted a doll to remind her of herself, there was still *Skipper,* and the even younger *Tutti. Barbie's* world was expanding, and covering all bases!

In 1968, the Mod reign was stronger than ever. A new word, "Psychedelic," was creeping up.

122. Short skirts, long straight hair and swingy earrings were the hallmark of fashion in this 1967 outfit, *Sunflower!*

123

124

Originally developed by the drug culture to describe a flashing light experience while on LSD, the word spilled over into teenage slang and meant "cool, and very modern." The top show of 1968 was "Rowan and Martin's Laugh-In." Hemlines were still creeping upwards and the boom children, now in college, were grooving to "Dance Concerts," a type of entertainment where you danced while a band played to a "mind blowing" light show.

Some teens, of course, would get caught up in the ever-blossoming "peace" ghettos of California and New York; some would die in the growing Vietnam war. Others would "alter consciousness" with the hallucinogenic

123. *Francie* had her own house and entertained *Black Francie!* Fashions are from left, 1971 *Zig-Zag Zoom* and 1966 *It's A Date.*

124. In 1971, Mattel had decided to offer another friend for *Francie* called *Becky.* The doll was made from the *Casey* head molds and was shown in catalogs. For some reason, the doll was never made. This box shows the logo for *Becky* that was sold for months. All this adds to the fun of *Barbie* collecting.

125. A 1969 and a 1968 *Talking Barbie* as they were originally sold. The 1968 doll in the case seems much more difficult to find.

126. A 1969 "Marlo Thomas" inspired *Barbie* models 1967 *Sparkle Squares*, while a 1967 *Twist 'N Turn Barbie* sports 1967s *Dancing Stripes*.

127. *P.J.* models *Check the Suit*, 1971, while *Stacey* with the 1969 short hair models 1970 *Lemon Kick*.

drugs available on any street corner. The largest group, thankfully, would just take the best from these trends and become "weekend" hippies, attending concerts dressed in wild clothing, then return back to the dorm to study for finals. Youth was asking to be wild and free. Many could not handle that much freedom!

1968 at Mattel saw the giant toy company dive headlong into the social issues of the day. *Barbie* got a black friend, *Christie.*

The statement this doll makes is really groundbreaking, for *Barbie* was crossing color lines to have a black best friend. *Christie* was a lovely girl who definitely was ethnically featured, but intelligent and pretty at the same time. In a country that just ten years before had separate drinking fountains for blacks and whites, this really was quite a step. The public found the connection wonderful, and blacks bought *Christie* as a companion for *Barbie.* It was a step in the right direction.

Also that year *Barbie* got a British friend, *Stacey.* Available as a platinum blonde or a dashing redhead, *Stacey* was Mod, but not quite as "far out" as *Twiggy.* Added to the dolls was a "talking" feature, similar to that used in the *Chatty Cathy* dolls of almost ten years earlier. The phrases uttered were typical teen sentences, performed by carefully selected actresses. The talking dolls would be around for a while, but proved troublesome as many broke easily. Today it is almost impossible to find one that still talks, even when sealed in the box.

Mention should be made that 1968 was the first year since 1961 that *Ken* was not available. The late 1960s were a hard time for teenage boys. An unfair war and even more unfair draft

128. Standard *Barbies.* Left is 1967, right is 1970. This doll was also offered as a mail-in offer for Campbell soup labels.

129. A 1969 *Talking P.J.* and *Talking Stacey.* The logo that year was "Everybody's Talking Barbie Talk." Even the fan club magazine was entitled *Barbie Talk.*

130. *Barbie* plays detective wearing *Intrigue*, a 1967 fashion that was illustrated with a pistol that was never produced.

"Julia," a nurse raising a son while widowed. What made the show meaningful was that not only was Julia black, her husband had been killed in the line of duty in Vietnam. The show was not seen as a black show, but a show about an ordinary family that just happened to be black. Ironically, Diahann Carroll would say that the last leading black lady on a TV show was "Beulah," a 1950 sitcom about a maid!

The lovely *Julia* doll joined the *Barbie* line of licensed friends. This author groups family, friends, celebrity friends and acquaintances differently than others, but *Julia* was not billed as *Barbie's* friend on the packaging, only that she could also wear *Barbie*-sized fashions. This is, to me, the criteria for categorizing the Mattel dolls in *Barbie's* world.

Another great licensed friend for *Barbie* in 1969 was the *Truly Scrumptious* doll. Made with *Francie's* head and *Barbie's* body, she reflected the Victorian look of the movie she was based on, *Chitty Chitty Bang Bang*.

With some fanfare *Ken* returned. Completely redesigned, this new *Ken* was huskier and hunkier. Teenage standards had evolved from the quiet "boy next door" type, into a more athletic and stockier type of young man. This new *Ken* had a completely redesigned face with longish side-parted "Edwardian" hair and a new wardrobe. This was necessary because *Ken* could not fit in his old wardrobe. (Some authorities feel that this is the reason *Ken* was absent in 1968).

system was forcing young men to either enlist, enroll in college (for the valued II-S deferment), or run away to Canada.

By eliminating *Ken* this very touchy year, Mattel avoided the obvious question of just what *Ken's* political beliefs were. Some news articles of the day picked up on this and one, in a mock interview with *Barbie*, asked her if he had run away to Canada. Always a lady, *Barbie* replied that yes, she missed him, but life goes on...

1969 saw another huge civil rights step for Mattel and *Barbie*. A television show called *Julia* debuted in 1968. By 1969, it was often rated number one of the week. Completely different, it featured the lovely Diahann Carroll as

131. A gorgeous 1968 *Talking Barbie* models *Little Bow Pink*. Hemlines were a real fashion statement in the late 1960s.

The Wonderful World of Barbie

MATTEL

133. In 1969 and 1970, Mattel aimed dolls at Spanish speaking youth in this *Spanish Talking Barbie* and *Ken.* They were moderately successful, but the time was not right for ethnic dolls.

134. 1970 saw blacks start to search for their African roots. This *Talking Christie* and *Talking Brad* mirror that trend in ethnic outfits. The dolls were a success and tied *Barbie* into another culture.

135. *Truly Scrumptious* was introduced in 1969 as a licensed friend for *Barbie* due to the popularity of the character in the film *Chitty Chitty Bang Bang.* The doll sported *Francie's* head on *Barbie's* body!

136. A 1970 Diahann Carroll as *Julia* with her fashion, *Burr, Fur.* This doll was representative of the move to a blending of cultures.

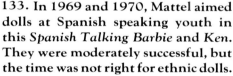

132. A 1969-1970 store display. This smart merchandising allowed these displays to act as a permanant salesman, always on duty to show off the product. These are very rare and highly sought after today.

137. 1970 *Walking Jamie* with blonde and red hair. Sears often sold exclusive dolls and clothing. These are more valuable and harder to find than the regular line of dolls.

138. The *Barbie Twist 'N Turn* dolls. Left: 1968, 1969, 1970 and 1971 with centered eyes. These shrink-wrapped dolls created the term "never removed from box," to indicate that the shrink-wrapping was still intact.

139. A late 1960s *Barbie House*, very MODern in style, hosts *Stacy* in 1970 *Rare Pair*, 1970 *Walking Jaime* and *Talking Ken* in 1970 *Bold Gold*. Finishing the happy group are a 1970 *Twist 'N Turn Barbie* in 1969 *Glo-Go* and 1969 *Talking P.J.* wearing 1966 *Print Aplenty*.

Also new in 1969 was a "new" friend for *Barbie*. The *Midge* head mold had been brought back in the guise of *P.J.*, billed as just a friend of *Barbie*. With her "peace" beads wrapping her twin ponytails, and an orangy floral mini, she was the epitome of late 1960s chic.

By mid 1969, both *Barbie* and *Francie* would get hairstyle updates. *Barbie's* new look was a shoulder length "flip" style with ends curled up and a spit curl over her eye. *Francie* had basically the same style except for thicker bangs and a shorter "flip."

140. *Ken* returned with Edwardian-look hair. He looked like he belonged on television's *Dark Shadows!*

141. Evening wear was still popular during the Mod period. Dress-up gowns such as *Silver Serenade* from 1971 and *Fab City* from 1969 were annual favorites.

142. After being absent in 1968, *Ken* returned newly designed in 1969, huskier and with an "Edwardian" hairstyle. Left is 1971 *V.I.P. Scene*. *Ken* models *Sea Scene*, 1971, and on right is 1970 *Big Business*.

143. 1970 *Living Barbie* was more posable than ever. Also issued the following year in a rare coin dot outfit, she had centered eyes, new for *Barbie*.

144. 1970 *Living Skipper* models *Wooly Winter* from the same year, while a 1970 *Living Barbie* dons 1971 *Super Scarf*. The mini skirt and "go go boots" were a popular look.

144

Both of these styles were based on the Marlo Thomas hairstyle from the television show "That Girl."

1970 saw the first disaster strike Mattel. The factory in Mexico, a primary manufacturing source since the Japanese factory was closed, was completely destroyed by a fire. The tragedy would signal the beginning of trouble for Mattel.

The dolls of 1970, however, were still of the highest quality. *Living Barbie* and *Living Skipper* were more posable than ever. A trade-in offer done the same way as the one in 1967 was arranged for *Skipper* dolls. For $1.99 a child could trade-in for new dolls.

Like before, the old dolls were donated to charity.

Christie, selling well, received her own boyfriend in *Brad*. Available in very "African" ethnic outfits, *Christie* and *Brad* symbolized the new black pride and awareness of African roots.

Sears, long a source of *Barbie* specials, made a friend for *Barbie*, *Walking Jamie*. Made from *Barbie* molds, her hair and coloring really made her seem different.

With the early 1970s came emphasis on hair care. *Francie* came with *Growin' Pretty Hair*, and as a *Hair Happenin's* doll with extra hairpieces. New for 1970 were more aquaintances

145. Late 1960s Sears *Talking Barbie* gift set. The artwork on these sets were a statement unto themselves. *Barbie's* outfit is trimmed in real mink!

146. *Barbie's Little Sister, Tutti* came in several play sets throughout the Mod period. Top is *Sundae Treat* and features *Todd*, her twin brother; left is *Walking My Dolly*, and right, *Night Night, Sleep Tight.*

147. The 1970s were very visible in this 1971 *Live Action Christie, Barbie* and *Ken.* Long straight center-parted hair and fringed psychedelic print outfits ushered in a new era.

for *Tutti. Nan 'N Fran*, a black doll and her doll; *Lori 'N Rori*, a blonde doll with a Teddy Bear; and *Angie 'N Tangie*, a brunette doll holding a blonde doll.

To satisfy Hispanic children, *Barbie* and *Ken* were available in 1970 as talking dolls that spoke Spanish! Often viewed today as "tokenism," these attempts to satisfy all children were actually quite advanced. Mattel was the only doll manufacturer that even acknowledged that America was made up of ALL ethnic backgrounds.

By 1971, the Mod movement had disintegrated, due mainly to the escalating Vietnam crisis. It seemed hard to party while high school friends were being drafted. The polarization

148

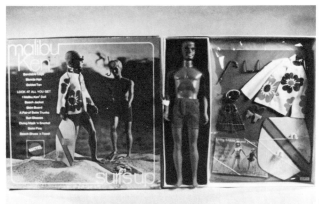

149

150

148. The *Malibu* dolls appeared in 1971. Featuring golden tans and long, straight blonde hair, they epitomized the "natural look" that was becoming popular in the early 1970s. 149. *Malibu Ken Surf's Up* gift set, a Sears exclusive, 1971. This set featured a very tan and blonde *Ken* that idealized the American dream of the "beach boy." 150. *Malibu Barbie* and *Ken* take to the sands in their beach buggy.

between those who thought we should be there an those who thought we should not even took its toll on fashion.

The "hippie," or someone who had great apathy, was becoming a national hero. Baby boom children were discovering that they could not control their own destiny as they once believed. This disenchantment led many to simply "drop out" of society. "Communes" were born, places where individuals who believed in shared love, peace and happiness could live together. Based on medieval principles of communal ownership, these places proved to be no utopia either as disease and drug use tainted the spoiled boom children.

During 1971, fashion adopted this "hippie" look, and suede fringe became the rage. Except for Italian movie stars who still sported false eyelashes and piled on curls, the "natural" look was "in." Long, straight hair, as seen on the children in the "Brady Bunch" on TV, was the newest look.

Live Action Barbie, Christie, P.J. and *Ken* were issued in 1971 in wild print clothing and heavy fringe. *Barbie, Christie* and *P.J.* had long, straight hair; *Ken* looked ready for Woodstock!

Some interesting new dolls appeared in 1971. A department store special *Barbie* with short, red hair and extra hairpieces was available, entitled *Barbie Hair Happenin's*. Also new were the *Malibu* dolls, available with gorgeous tans and California blonde straight hair a la Cheryl Tiegs, the top model of the day. An interesting *Francie* with an off-the-face flip style hairdo was also issued. *Skipper* got a new friend, *Fluff,* and both *Living Barbie* and *Living Skipper* were modified!

And the beat goes on...

151

152

151. The incoming "granny gown" craze can be seen in this 1972 *Barbie with Growin' Pretty Hair.* Contrasted next to her is the last of the Mod dolls, the 1971 version in a Mod-inspired dress. Times were changing!

152. One of the last of the TV families that exuded the "apple pie" Americanism was the "Brady Bunch." Starting in 1969, this show is important to *Barbie* collectors because Maureen McCormick, playing Marcia Brady and shown seated third from the left, was the child in several of the late 1960s *Barbie* commercials. Cindy Brady, (Susan Olsen) looked just like *Tutti, Barbie's Little Sister.*

VI. The Passive Seventies (1972-1976)

The registered trademarks, the trademarks and the copyrights appearing in italics within this chapter belong to Mattel, Inc., unless otherwise noted.

The early 1970s were uncertain years for the Handlers and Mattel. In January 1972, Mattel reported an unprecedented loss of 30 million dollars in revenue. By June the Handlers' lawyer, Seymour Rosenburg, would be gone, after selling off 80,000 shares of company stock for two million dollars.

In 1973, the Handlers were forced out of management and Art Spears, executive vice president in charge of operations, became president. The Securities Exchange Commission would later claim that during 1970-71, Mattel's managers had grossly violated standard accounting practices to gain much needed capital.

It was reported in an article in *Savvy, The Magazine for Executive Women*, May 1980, that this whole situation ended in 1978 with Ruth Handler and Seymour Rosenburg pleading no contest to ten counts of securities and mail fraud. She was fined, along with Rosenburg, to pay $57,000 and sentenced to serve 2500 hours of community service.

Time has made everyone evaluate just what did happen. In my opinion, the simple truth is that Mattel had growing pains. Hindsight points out that questionable advice coupled with

adverse business conditions caused trouble to one of the most creative ladies in the doll world. It truly was the end of an era.

All of these problems, of course, affected the *Barbie* program. In 1972, for the first time, there were no fashion booklets packaged with the dolls. A simple move like this could save millions in production costs.

Actually, I feel that the dolls from 1972 and 1973 did not show the lack of quality the dolls and fashions from 1974-1976 would show. Changes may not have "caught up" yet because of a wealth of pre-designed dolls, clothes and accessories.

The year 1972 saw the introduction of *Walk Lively Ken, Barbie, Steffie* and *Miss America*. Laura Lee Shaefer, Miss America of 1972, was one of the most visible Miss Americas ever. She promoted her doll on Kellogg's Corn Flakes with a special mail-in offer, minus the walking stand that came with the dolls sold in stores.

153. *Malibu Ken* and *Barbie* on their way to a peace march! Dolls dressed like this bring back memories to the baby boom children who did it all.

Malibu P.J. was added to the *Malibu* line of dolls that year. Her head was made from the *Steffie* molds. That mold is used even in 1987 for *Barbie's* new friend, *Whitney!*

Teenagers were into activities, and the 1972 dolls had what would be called "busy" hands, or hands that opened and closed, allowing them to hold objects packaged with them like a

154. Although dated 1972 and available 1973 and 1974, this paper doll showed the earlier "talking" doll, obviously better quality for a photograph.

155. *Walk Lively Barbie and Ken, 1972.* These dolls are the epitome of early 1970s fashions. *Barbie's* long, straight, center-parted hair and bell-bottoms are typical period fashions, as are *Ken's* plaid pants!

TV set or a suitcase. The talking feature was still popular that year; all the "busy dolls" came in talking versions except *Francie*, mainly because her body was too small to hold the mechanism.

Available in "busy" form were *Barbie*, *Ken*, *Steffie* and *Francie*. *Talking Busy Dolls* were, *Barbie*, *Ken* and *Steffie*. The year 1972 saw the introduction of other "action" dolls, with *Pose 'N' Play Skipper* who had "swinging-free arms," and her tomboy friend, *Tiff*, a very rare doll today. *Tiff* was made from the *Fluff* molds and came dressed in jeans and a white tee shirt.

Barbie had to have some glamour so a new version of *Barbie* was added to the line, *Barbie with Growin' Pretty Hair*. It was interesting to note that "granny gowns," the official "hippie" dress-up clothing, was utilized for *Barbie*. Also big that year was the "prairie look," evident in both *Barbie* and *Francie* outfits. American fashion

---

156. "The Partridge Family," starring Shirley Jones, David Cassidy and Susan Dey, exemplified the typical "flower power" family of the early 1970s. *Movie Star News* photograph.

157. 1973 was the year of women's rights. *Barbie* made a wonderful statement by becoming a doctor! In the early 1960s, she was allowed only to be a nurse.

158. A very rare *Put ons and Pets* outfit from 1972. This wonderful period outfit featured "hot pants," the latest youth craze. *Barbie's* dog is a great addition to this ensemble!

157

158

159. 100th Anniversary Montgomery
Wards' *Barbie.* This was supposed to
be the "original" *Barbie* (a very mis-
used term), but actually was an exact
reproduction of a number five doll.

was really at a low point as far as glamour was concerned.

1972 was a boring year for American pop culture. Vietnam was a despised venture; "causes" were dying rapidly as teens realized that the government had misled them about the major issues of the day. "Apathy" was the password of the early 1970s.

The only highpoint of the year was that an old established firm, Montgomery Ward, was celebrating its 100th anniversary. Long a source of gift sets and other specials for *Barbie*. Wards had Mattel reissue the "original" *Barbie* doll for its anniversary celebration. Made to look like the number five ponytail, this doll is much sought after today by ardent collectors. Even Mattel thought of this doll as the "original" doll, for she really was one of the first of the heavily mass-marketed dolls. This thinking even went unchanged in 1984, for Mattel publicity shots showed a number five *Barbie*, in 8in (20cm) by 10in (25cm) glossies as the "original" *Barbie*. This has added much to the confusion with the general public about the value of the early dolls.

1973 saw an American obsession with hair. It was a natural thing. Those in established jobs could not wear the long, straight hairdos associated with

160. *Talking Busy Barbie*. These dolls were interesting in that they had a "serf," or peasant haircut, "hot pants," and the "busy" hands that could open and close.

161. In 1973, *Barbie* got a new friend, *Quick Curl Kelley*. *Francie* was on her way out, but made a last try as a brunette.

162. *Quick Curl Barbie* was so popular, she was issued in the gift set distributed by Burbank Toys in the United Kingdom. An extra outfit was included.

the "flower children." Men in "corporate" jobs, thought by many to be part of the "establishment" and over 30, could not have the long "shag" haircut made famous by David Cassidy on "The Partridge Family." In fact, the *Barbie* and *Ken* of this era could well be the Keith and Laurie Partridge (Laurie played by Susan Dey) from this show. Laurie, with her long, straight hair and Keith, with his flowered shirts and shag cut, were the perfect uninvolved teen couple.

Mattel responded to this trend by issuing *Mod Hair Ken*. The musicals, "Godspell" and "Jesus Christ, Superstar" of 1973 gave young Americans historical and biblical reasons why long stringy hair was okay.

"Quick Curl Hair," the big feature on all the dolls that year, could go from straight and flat, to fluffy and curly with a twist of a wand. The secret was a wire fiber rooted into the hair. The lead dolls were *Quick Curl Barbie*, *Skipper*, *Francie* (as a rare brunette) and *Miss America*. *Barbie* got a new *Quick Curl* friend in *Kelley*, a lovely redhead made form the *Steffie* molds. *Malibu Christie*, a black doll, joined the *Sun Set* that year.

The company troubles were evident in 1973, for leftover stock was issued in "baggies," (plastic bags with cardboard tops), containing old dolls.

1974 was an interesting year in *Barbie* doll history. This was *Barbie's* 16th birthday. Actually, if you count backwards, only 15 years had passed since *Barbie* was introduced at Toy Fair in 1959. Eager to recapture lost revenues, the new leadership at Mattel

163. The "busy" series of 1972-73 found another new friend for *Barbie* in Busy Steffie. 164. Early 1970s *Barbie* fashions reflected the looks of the day with longer skirts, the ever popular miniskirt and, of course, formal wear. 165. Charlotte Johnson, the designer of all the *Barbie* fashions the entire time the Handlers were at Mattel, came the closest yet in the early 1970s to a name credit. The packaging of some deluxe outfits featured a mention of "C.J." who traveled "world wide" to find fabrics for *Barbie* fashions.

used the patent date, 1958, as the official date of *Barbie's* birth. Because *Barbie* was around 16 years old, the tie-in was a natural.

Unfortunately, quality was not the goal of Mattel in 1974, profit was. In order to stay afloat, it was necessary to design catchy, glittery products that did not cost much to produce. The *Sweet 16 Barbie* lacked even the essentials of earlier dolls. Gone were the rich eyelashes, rooted in the plastic, and the hand done hairstyles. In their place was cheaper vinyl with poorly painted features and a "shag" cut that unfortunately, was the "in" style.

In all fairness, the *Sweet 16 Barbie*, when one looks backwards, is a lovely doll that looks 16! Earlier dolls had become so "couture" that *Barbie* could have easily been 35 under all that makeup! This doll capitalized on the fresh face look of current cover girls like Cheryl Tiegs, whose "clean make-up" face glowed from Sears catalogs. In a last ditch effort to trim costs further, wrist tags were discontinued, a move which again saved several million dollars a year for Mattel. Besides, the current customer of *Barbie*, younger and less sophisticated than teens of the early 1960s, did not care about such amenities.

New in 1974 was the *Sports Set*. These dolls included *Sun Valley Barbie*, a ski queen with a golden tan like Suszi Chaffee; *Sun Valley Ken*, her male counterpart; *Newport Barbie*, dressed

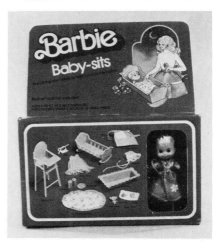

166. In 1974, a year early, *Barbie* turned "Sweet 16." A special promotional doll with extra outfits consisting of "cut offs" and a "tank top" was issued. This set was bought in Canada and features both French and English on the packaging. 167. 1974 *Sports Set* dolls. *Sun Valley Barbie* and *Newport Barbie*, made from the *Malibu* dolls. 168. In 1974, Sears had a *Barbie Baby Sits* exclusive, using the baby from Mattel's *Sunshine Family*. This was the first issue of such a set since 1965. The set could give girls a chance to play "mommy" with *Barbie*, a role which never suited the doll!

169. The 1975 Olympic Games resulted in a 2 million dollar promotional tie-in with Mattel. *Barbie* wore the gold medal of many countries including Canada, with its Maple Leaf. The set, center, is a Sears exclusive. The paper doll shows *Cara* and *Curtis*, *Barbie's* black friends.

170. 1975 *Free Moving Cara* and *Barbie*. The quality reflects a company in crisis.

for sailing; and *Yellowstone Kelley*, ready for camping.

Of note in 1974 was the issue of *Busy Steffie* stock in a plastic bag, titled, *Babs*. (Babs had been the name of earlier *Barbie* competitors.)

Still eager to capture the collector, Montgomery Wards issued a *Mod Hair Ken* dressed in an exclusive tuxedo, of the "tacky" variety one would wear to "show off" in the mid 1970s!

Americans were bored out of their minds in 1975. After five years of doing nothing, they were ready to celebrate. The 1975 Olympic Games gave them just such a chance. Never in the history of the Olympics had there been such a fanfare! Mattel tied into the campaign with a 2 million dollar advertising budget! *Gold Medal Barbie*, complete with her award medal, appeared in the stores as early as January 1975. Usually Mattel launched new dolls in the late Spring.

The doll was a regular *Malibu* doll, (every athlete has a tan, of course!), dressed in a one-piece red, white and blue swimsuit. Mail-in coupons allowed the child to send for a record book to keep track of the events and an iron-on shield for shirt or jacket.

A few weeks later other *Gold Medal* dolls reached the market, and included a *Barbie Skier*, *Barbie Skater*, *Ken Skier* and a *P.J. Gymnast*. Separate Olympic outfits were available for the almost defunct *Francie*, and *Skipper* as well. Sears had exclusive dolls with extra clothes for post Olympic events. Whitman issued a special sports theme paper doll book.

These dolls are especially noteworthy because they mirrored Mattel's new management philosophy that *Barbie* SHOULD have an identity that girls can relate to. Children of this period were far less imaginative than

171. The *Now Look Ken*. Did we REALLY look like that? It is hard to believe that is *Ken* beneath that hair! Dolls like this tell the story of American pop culture so very well!

172. *Francie* sported a new hairdo in 1971, known to collectors as *No Bangs Francie*. This particular version is extremely rare and is valued at over $500, out-of-box!

173. A rare *Growing-Up Skipper* fashion. This controversial doll grew breasts when her arm was turned!

174. The incredibly poor quality of this *Barbie plus 3* set available in 1975 is proof that Mattel was having problems. The doll is a nightmarish imitation of *Barbie*, and the clothing is "goodwill box" quality!

their predecessors and needed a visual, active role model. The new *Gold Medal Barbie*, made from the smiling *Stacey* molds, had a confident, secure personality that post Vietnam children needed. Many of these children were not getting that security at home the way the "Leave It to Beaver" generation had. Today's mother was "burned out," either from the drug culture or peace causes. *Barbie* was offereing these children a fresh start at life, untainted by years they did not help shape or understand.

Also introduced in 1975 were *Free Moving Barbie, Ken, P.J.* and the black *Cara* and *Curtis* dolls. The need for *Barbie* to be blonde and white was still there, but her friends could be black. It would be another five years before *Barbie* could be seen as belonging to other cultures.

The big controversy of the year was a doll called *Growing Up Skipper*. With a twist of her arm, her budding breasts sprouted, and she grew 3/4th of an inch (2cm)! Every newspaper in the country carried stories about the "immorality" of the doll, but in reality, children loved her. She was a huge success to children who saw the natural development of *Skipper* as healthy.

Also added to the *Quick Curl* line for 1975 was *Quick Curl Cara*, a black doll. Department stores got a lovely new doll, *Hawaiian Barbie*, made from the heavily used *Steffie* molds.

1975 was the beginning of a turning point in Mattel profits after the lean years of the early 1970s. Revenues were coming in sufficiently to launch an exciting new line for 1977!

1976 started off with a new logo for *Barbie*. Most collectors, myself included, do not think the new logo tells the fashion image of *Barbie* as well as the old, script logo.

For 1976, the *Quick Curl* dolls were issued in deluxe sets with "falls,"

or hairpieces that could be attached to create glamorous new play possibilities. Long hair for men was still in style (although would go out with a "snip" next year), and Mattel issued *Now Look Ken* with super long rooted hair.

For those traditionally minded, *Ballerina Barbie* was available. Dressed in a typical ballet costume, her black friend, *Cara*, also was ready for practice.

Growing Up Skipper got a new friend, *Growing Up Ginger*, basically the same doll with dark hair; *Barbie* and *Skipper* both got Bicentennial outfits featuring colonial patriots marching for freedom.

The passive seventies were, thankfully, drawing to a close! Just ahead was the razzle dazzle of a new beat.

175. This Whitman paper doll set featured genuine *Barbie* fashions. While the quality was not as good as previous years, the theme selection was quite interesting.

VII. Disco Daze (1977-1979)

The registered trademarks, the trademarks and the copyrights appearing in italics within this chapter belong to Mattel, Inc., unless otherwise noted.

By the late 1970s, the baby boomers were restless. Having spent the last ten years involved in peace marches, sit-ins and demonstrations, they were weary of "causes." Haight-Ashbury, the California haven for "hippies" and "flower children" was overrun with disease, crime and poverty. Suddenly the "establishment" did not look so bad after all.

Little by little, women began to dress up. Gradually at first, because it was not easy to surrender those jeans and army-navy store jackets, but slowly glamour began to return.

In New York, nightclubs were opening up that were devoted to playing the elaborate music of late 1970s. That music was "DISCO!" Originally played in Latin clubs as a throwback to calypso, the music spread to the black clubs, the gay clubs, and then to all America. Soon "chic" places such as "Studio 54" opened in New York, and almost overnight it was fashionable to dress up and go out! The late 1970s, like the Roaring Twenties, came right after a war, Vietnam, and people were ready to let the corks pop. They were tired of Richard Nixon, acid rock and long dragging bell-bottoms. Suddenly people wanted to look plastic! Bianca Jagger and Calvin Klein became the new "celebs" to watch; a lovely baby boomer named Farrah Fawcett-Majors

was the star of a TV show called, "Charlie's Angels." The impact that Farrah had on our culture was similar to that of Marilyn Monroe in the 1950s.

Her dazzling wide smile and sun-streaked hair were the epitome of late 1970s' glamour. Suddenly Bloomingdales became the "in" spot to shop. Times were changing very quickly.

Mattel spotted this trend and responded. By 1977, most of their economic problems left over from the previous years were under control. *Barbie* could once again be a fashion leader and representative of today's young women.

With much fanfare, Mattel announced the arrival of *Superstar Barbie!* The resemblance to Farrah was amazing. Not only that, but her arms bent in a glamourous pose and she wore jewelry, absent from the dolls during the product safety code years. Her dress was long and swingy and she sported a sparkly boa! With her came *Superstar Fashions* that were miles away from the outfits one would have worn only a handful of years before!

---

176. This *Promotional Superstar Barbie*, with face modeled after Farrah Fawcett-Majors, launched a new era for *Barbie* in 1977.

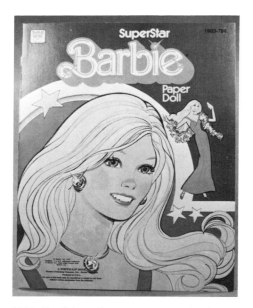

177. *Barbie's* glamorous new look was captured in this paper doll from Whitman, 1977.

178. Special outfits for *Superstar Barbie* were issued in 1977 that signaled the return of real quality to Mattel. On the left is *Romantic White*, right is *Silver Shimmer*.

Adding to the glamour was a *Star 'Vette* that allowed *Barbie* to arrive at the disco in style. Not mentioned in the company catalogs was a *Promotional Superstar Barbie* that had a slinky, glitterly dress and white rabbit stole. Afraid to push the new look too far, the 1977 catalog is mainly made up of carryovers from other years. Also, Mattel was just getting back on its feet.

In 1978, the disco scene was in full swing. Every major city had dance clubs that were like speakeasies. One pulled up in a fancy car and made a grand entrance. Dance contests were every place, with prizes that ranged from dinner for two at a local "hot spot" to a trip around the world.

For teenage boys, this spelled trouble. Suddenly the best dancer in the class had all the dates, and not the best football player. Clothing long labeled as "sisified" was in style, and "in" boys spent hours at the hairstylist (barbershop was an old man's term!) getting the latest razor cut. The style-conscious male was getting all the attention. The jock was out.

To meet this trend, Mattel issued, in 1978, *Superstar Ken*. Dressed in a navy blue polyester jumpsuit with flare pants, he also sported "shades" (sunglasses to the unknowing) and much jewelry. A deluxe set was issued with both dolls in the box that looks like it was dropped out of Studio 54 in

179. The back of the *Superstar Barbie Fashions'* boxes had spectacular artwork that told the story of *Barbie's* disco nights.

180. By 1978, the *Superstar Barbie Fashions* were even more glamorous as disco swept America. Better ideas and fabrics were used this year, but the outfits simply had a stock number and were not named in the catalog.

New York! *Superstar Christie, Barbie's* black friend joined the party.

Another lead doll that year was *Fashion Photo Barbie*, which utilized the superstar molds and took *Barbie* back into the world of modeling. Her picture could be taken while she twirled a la Loretta Young in a chiffon gown.

Joining the *Barbie* family of friends in 1977-1978 were the Osmonds, *Donny, Marie* and *Jimmy*. The "Donny and Marie" show was also taking Americans back to glamour, yet discreetly, every Friday evening as Marie announced that she was "just a little bit country," while Donny was "just a little bit rock and roll." The dolls were lovely and cleverly made with definite resemblances to the stars. Gone, however, was the "friend" tie-in to *Barbie*,

as they were just the same size, yet, in my opinion, not part of the *Barbie* family. Added to this in the 1978 Mattel catalog were *Kitty O'Neil*, a deaf race car driver, *Kate Jackson*, "Sabrina" on "Charlie's Angels" and *Cheryl Ladd*, who replaced Farrah in that same show as Jill Monroe's sister, Chris. Again, I do not consider these dolls part of the *Barbie* family because no mention was made in the campaign or on the boxes about them being friends of *Barbie*, only that the same clothing would fit them.

1978 saw many "specials" that the collector should try to add to his/her collection. A *Malibu Barbie Fashion Combo*, sold in the Philadelphia area only at Best Products, was a gift set featuring a *Malibu Barbie* and extra

181

182

clothes. Another great set was *Beautiful Bride Barbie*, available only in department stores and featured the new superstar molds.

Even True Value Hardware stores had a *Superstar Barbie Fashion Change-Abouts* set that was only available the month before Christmas, 1978, and featured a doll with a mix-and-match wardrobe. A set called *Superstar Barbie in the Spotlight* appeared as a department store special and was available in two versions.

In 1977 and 1978 an 18in (46cm) *Supersize Barbie* appeared in the stores, along with the black version, *Supersize Christie*. It failed to attract attention, despite the introduction of a department store special, *Supersize Bridal Barbie*, because even though the doll was incredibly well made, the public just did not think of *Barbie* as that size. Tried as an experiment because another fashion doll, *Candy*, had been doing well in both sizes, Mattel realized with mixed emotions that *Barbie* was petite and not that tall. These dolls, the failures as it were, will be valuable to future collectors because of their short shelf life.

By 1979, things were slowing down a bit. Romance had begun to combine with glamour. Mattel issued *Kissing Barbie*, a doll that could pucker her lips and plant a kiss on *Ken*. The doll was frilly and feminine, and not very popular. A department store special with an extra gown was issued but it,

181. **The face of the late 1970s, Farrah Fawcett-Majors. Her glowing tan and toothy grin, along with her signature hairstyle, would launch a new doll and a new era for** *Barbie.* **American girls would copy her look for the next ten years!** *Movie Star News photograph.*

182. **The movie** *Saturday Night Fever* **(Paramount, 1977), would propel dancing and dressing to new heights. The classic film portrayed a young dancer (John Travolta) using his talents for escape to a better life. The fashions and crazes it would create lasted for years!** *Movie Star News photograph.*

183. By 1978, *Superstar Barbie* was joined with *Superstar Ken*, in this gift set, available only in selected stores. *Superstar Ken* took the concept of *Barbie's* boyfriend away from all-American and into the realm of sophisticated nightlife.

184. *Superstar Ken and Barbie* exemplified the return of dressing up and going out in America. They were the epitome of the "beautiful people."

185. Many licensed products helped familiarize the new face of *Barbie* to the public. Ambassador Greetings, a division of Hallmark, issued two greeting cards with the new doll, and Golden Books published a *Barbie* fantasy featuring the new *Superstar Barbie*.

186. Special gift sets were available in 1978 for *Superstar Barbie* such as this set on the left for department stores called *Superstar Barbie in the Spotlight* and the set on the right, *Superstar Barbie Fashion Change-abouts* available at True Value Hardware.

too, failed to meet expectations.

Ballerina Barbie, however, was made for the girl with other dreams, and added to the department store special called *Ballerina Barbie on Tour*, which featured the costumes from "The Nutcracker." Even Sears had an exclusive outfit with a record for the doll.

The lead doll of the year was a tame *Pretty Changes Barbie*, interesting only in that her hair was short, which was rare. With her came a blonde "fall" and a brunette wig. The quality was just not there, and her popularity was not that of the *Superstar Barbie* dolls. Clearly Americans wanted the type of woman who was exciting and glamorous.

Barbie's Little Sister, Skipper, became a teenager this year, with a new, grown-up image that, too, would prove unpopular. Notice also that the 1977-1979 lines were basically small compared to other years that would follow. Mattel was still, as was the nation, floundering to find itself.

Many young Americans will always remember the period from 1977-1979 as a fast moving time of dancing, glamour, bright lights and excitement. The problem was that change was so overdue, that it was happening too rapidly! Mattel, afraid to take too many chances after the "fall" of a few years before, was playing safe with a smaller line that covered all bases. Glamour queen, disco star, fashion

187. Something had to pay for all the glamourous nights at the disco, and in 1978, *Barbie* resumed her career as a fashion model with *Fashion Photo Barbie*. 188. The *Malibu* dolls had been best sellers for years. This set, *Malibu Barbie Fashion Combo*, was sold in Philadelphia only at Best Products. The collector should always be watching for specials such as this, as they are rapidly discontinued.

model, romantic heroine, all were adjectives to describe the *Barbie* doll of the late 1970s. Just ahead were the energetic 1980s, and a bit slower pace!

189. *Donny and Marie Osmond* entertain *Barbie* and *Ken* on *The Donny and Marie TV Show* set. Dolls are all wearing *Donny and Marie* fashions. *Marie's* hair styled by author.

190. The disco period had to have some tradition for *Barbie*. She was issued as a department store special bride in these two dolls, available in 1976-77 on the left, with real rooted eyelashes, and the "old" *Barbie* face. Also marketed in 1978 was the new *Superstar Barbie* dressed as a bride. Both were called *Beautiful Bride Barbie*.

191. The success of a competing fashion doll that was issued in two sizes hastened Mattel to issue *Barbie* in this 18in (46cm) size. As a department store special bride in 1978, she still did not capture the market intended. The petite image of *Barbie* was impossible to break.

192. By 1979, quality was being seen everywhere in Mattel products. This matching outfit set for *Barbie* and *Ken* called *City Sophisticate* came in solid cardboard boxes with clothing labels and the old trappings of quality that made Mattel famous in the 1960s.

193. Despite the glamour emphasis, ballerinas and brides were still popular with little girls, especially those under five. *Ballerina Barbie on Tour* was a popular 1979 department store special that featured the doll and costumes from "The Nutcracker."

194. Romance entered into the disco scene with the new found popularity of the romance novel. *Kissing Barbie* on the left was issued for mass-market stores (this doll has the rare banged hair-do), and on the right as a department store special with extra gown.

195. Unusual because of her short, blonde hair, this *Pretty Changes Barbie* of 1979 helped teach a young girl about hairstyles. Her popularity was not as great as anticipated because little girls pictured *Barbie* with long blonde hair.

VIII.
The Energetic Eighties (1980-1989)

The registered trademarks, the trademarks and the copyrights appearing in italics wihtin this chapter belong to Mattel, Inc., unless otherwise noted.

By 1980, America's love affair with disco was winding down. Many reasons can be cited for this, most notable being that so many people wanted to enter the "big" name clubs in major cities, that the doormen of these establishments were picking and choosing who could grace the dance floor. Americans were simply not used to being denied access to someplace they were willing to pay exorbitant sums of money to enter. These high prices were another deterrent to the continuation of the club culture started in the late 1970s.

Tired of wearing jeans since Vietnam, American women were not ready to stop dressing up. Even men were wearing colors once deemed "unmasculine" and the dolls reflect these trends.

Mattel in 1980 released *Beauty Secrets Barbie*, billed as having the longest hair ever on a *Barbie* doll. Her main feature was that her wrists were jointed so that she could hold a brush. A panel on her back made her arms move realistically. Along with her was a black version, named *Beauty Secrets Christie*, which was basically the same doll.

Men were starting to get into shape. Of course, all that disco dancing had

196. The 1980s show *Barbie* a proud, black woman astronaut, setting an example for everyone that "We girls CAN do anything...right, *Barbie*?"

197. The roller disco craze allowed American families to dance together on skates! *Roller Skating Barbie* and *Ken* from 1980 strut their stuff!

198. A rare *Beauty Secrets Barbie* store display. One hundred of these special plastic bubble displays were sent at random to Mattel accounts. This display was found in Hartford, Connecticut. Grooming and glamour were obsessions with American teens.

199. *Barbie* doll collectors have formed groups which meet annually to swap dolls and ideas. These convention souvenirs show a 1980 *Beauty Secrets Barbie* wearing a banner that says "21 Years of *Barbie*." The doll on the right is a specially dressed 1984 *Loving You Barbie* for *Barbie's* 25th birthday in New York. The center doll is a *Sun Gold Malibu Barbie*, dressed for the 1986 Phoenix, Arizona, convention.

already started to chip away at the flab, and men seemed eager to join the burgeoning health movement. A new *Sport and Shave Ken*, was out that year. Billed as "all man," (a phrase that would die out with the word "macho"), his main feature was a magic marker beard that could be "shaved off" with water, His extra "dress" outfit was a pair of sweat pants, sneakers and polo shirt. The advertising even dared to show a little boy joining in the fun of playing with this doll, but *Ken* was still sold in the "doll aisle," making him still taboo for most boys.

Available were *Black Barbie* and *Hispanic Barbie*. Mattel still felt the need to have their unquestionable ethnic backgrounds on the boxes.

Two of the most interesting new dolls for 1980 were *Super Teen Skipper* and her boyfriend, *Scott*. Could it be possible that *Barbie's Little Sister, Skipper*, had actually grown up? As previously mentioned, the big controversy over *Grownin' Up Skipper* had sent her back to childhood. Suddenly the psychologists at Mattel felt that the timing was right for another try at "teendom" for *Skipper*. Little girls were more eager than ever to grow up. Many fourth graders knew more about hair and makeup than their mothers did. Perhaps a teenage *Skipper* would work.

Accompanied by a skateboard, *Skipper* also had a ball gown! Her boyfriend, *Scott*, looked very much like "Bobby" on *"The Brady Bunch,"* (played by Michael Lookingland). In order to succeed, *Scott* had to be "hunky" enough to attract *Skipper*, but not overly sexy to offend anyone. In my opinion, he WAS too sexy. Children who had identified with *Skipper* being younger did not want to see the threat of a boyfriend in her life just yet. *Scott* was rapidly discontinued, and *Skipper* was eased back into the role of hoping she would "grow up" just like *Barbie*.

By late 1980, Americans had found a way to incorporate disco into their lives again, this time as a family! The new hero of the day was, of all places, the local roller skating rink! Now everyone in the family could spin, twirl and gyrate together on skates. This truly united disco music, exercise and the family as never before.

The movie industry responded to this "fad" by issuing catchy movies about roller skating that ranged from great to awful. Memorable was *Roller Boogie* with Linda Blair (remember her years earlier as Reagan in *The Exorcist?*) spinning more than just her head! *Skatetown U.S.A.* rapidly followed.

Mattel rapidly responded to this by issuing later in the year a beautiful set of dolls, *Roller Skating Barbie* and *Roller Skating Ken*. Dressed in matching, well-designed outfits, their skates were very lifelike. Unfortunately, America was moving at a rapid pace, on the rink and off, and the dolls were not around long.

Interestingly, 1980 was the 21st birthday of the *Barbie* doll. The occasion was completely ignored officially by Mattel, who was worried about taking *Barbie* out of the realm of a teenager. The media, however, played up this event with much publicity. Soon, however, with the arrival of "Dynasty" on ABC television, older women would be glamorized.

In 1980, the average little girl thought *Barbie* was 16-21. By 1987, some girls pictured her as old as 40! This was easy to do when Jaclyn Smith and Farrah Fawcett approached this age. *Barbie's* 25th birthday would not be ignored.

1981 saw glamour more popular

Introducing My First Barbie: The new Barbie doll designed for younger girls.

200. Mattel, eager to expand its market to the younger child, issued *My First Barbie* in 1981. This ad, from *Family Circle*, shows actress Heather O'Rourke with her doll.

201. Mattel wanted to encourage the collecting of *Barbie* dolls by adults, and acquired a list of collectors. These people were sent company catalogs annually, as well as a Christmas card, such as this one from 1981. As the number of collectors grew from hundreds to thousands, this practice had to be discontinued!

202. As disco music died down, country music revved up! In 1981, *Western Ken* and *Barbie*, and horses *Midnight* and *Dallas* appeared. *Barbie* could "wink" a hello and carried an autographed album cover. Her hairdo is a copy of Farrah Fawcett's style in "Charlie's Angels," a popular TV show.

203. Blacks had always viewed *Barbie* as white. In 1980, a *Black Barbie* was introduced. By 1982, *Magic Curl Barbie* was black, making no mention of such on the packaging, thus giving *Barbie* many identities for children of all races. Naturally *Barbie* needed *Ken*, so he, too, was issued in a black version.

than ever. Nighttime soaps such as "Dallas" and "Dynasty" were making "costume" dressing an art. Matching coats and hats to dresses were making a comeback that had not been seen since Joan Crawford in *Mildred Pierce* in 1945. Nolan Miller, the designer on the "Dynasty" set envisioned himself much like Adrian, THE designer of the 1930s, and wanted American women to look like movie stars. Mattel issued *Golden Dream Barbie* with the "Quick Curl" hair feature used once before and gave her a *Dream'Vette* to ride in.

Some Americans were finding a new thrill in country music, as a

204. Mattel created "specials" for department stores and specialty shops over the years. Usually including the lead doll for the year, something extra was added such as an additional outfit or item for the child. These sets rapidly disappear from store shelves and increase in value to the collector. From left, 1980 *Beauty Secrets Barbie Pretty Reflections*, 1981 *Golden Dream Barbie Golden Nights*, 1982 *Pink and Pretty Barbie* and 1983 *Twirley Curls Barbie*. 205. Additional department store special sets. 1984 *Loving You Barbie*, 1985 *Happy Birthday Barbie* and 1986 *Tropical Barbie Deluxe Gift Set*. 206. *Pink and Pretty Barbie* from 1982 sits at her *Electronic Piano*, a fabulous accessory that actually played! The framed picture was available by mail from Mattel.

207. 1983 *Barbie & Friends Gift Set.* In this rare set of three dolls in the same box, *Barbie* was dressed like a "Valley Girl" and *P.J.* was explained to be her cousin.

208. 1983 *Barbie & Ken Campin' Out Set.* Not since 1977 did *Barbie* and *Ken* come packaged together. These sets were not mass marketed and were available only in the western half of the United States.

statement away from the materialism of the "Dynasty" type of lifestyle. Singers such as Dolly Parton were crossing the line. Since many disco singers were one hit only stars, she and others like her were gaining in popularity. Country music was crossing over on the pop charts and getting away from its "hick" image.

The timing was right for *Western Barbie* and friends! An unusual doll, this *Barbie* could "wink" at the audience, and came with "album cover" pictures for her to autograph. Her hair was so VERY much a Farrah copy that it underwent three changes in one year. Her horse, *Dallas*, was issued, along with *Western Ken* and *Skipper.*

New for 1981 was the *My First Barbie.* In a brilliant ad campaign, Mattel showed a very young child (Heather O'Rourke of later *Poltergeist* fame!) playing safely with a *Barbie* doll that had smooth legs and special clothes. The thinking was to capture the younger market and keep it until the child "grew up," something which was happening by fourth grade. As more and more publicity arrived about the "collectibility" of the older *Barbie* dolls, little girls began to play with *Barbie* longer; having many older dolls gave one a kind of "status" with school chums. Fortunately for Mattel, today older girls are still displaying some of the more collectible dolls in their rooms as "shelf dolls," thus giving doll collecting respectability.

The 1980s saw a major breakthrough for civil rights. Up until these years, the public had viewed *Barbie* as white. As mentioned previously, a black *Francie* doll had been rebuffed by blacks themselves in the late 1960s. *Christie, Barbie's* black friend had been a success in her own right. Issued as a "companion" doll to *Barbie,* it was

209. 1984 was the 25th birthday of the *Barbie* doll! Mattel launched a major publicity campaign, such as this ad from *Playthings Magazine*, February 1984, proclaiming that an American legend had turned 25!

obvious that black children would play more with *Christie* as in examples such as *Superstar Christie*.

Finally, a breakthrough came in 1980 when *Black Barbie* was introduced. With a phrase borrowed from the TV show "Good Times." *Black Barbie* was "dynamite." Blacks were joyous to receive *Black Barbie* into their households, as they were no longer trying to be white to succeed in a white dominated society, but were accepting being black as something to be proud of.

The real breakthrough came with *Magic Curl Barbie*, an historic moment, for gone was the word "black" on the box. Both the white and black versions of this doll were identically dressed and packaged! For the first time in 23 years, *Barbie* was available as either black or white, without finding a "place" for the black version. This

trend continues today. ALL the lead dolls every year have a black and white issue. This is a great step for blacks in the US, and *Barbie* helped do it!

The disco craze was not fully dead, nor by any means was the health kick. Mattel issued *Fashion Jeans Barbie* and *Fashion Jeans Ken* in pink shirts and designer jeans complete with *Barbie's* own signature on the back pocket a la Calvin Klein and Gloria Vanderbilt. The newest upscale way to still wear blue jeans was to wear designer ones! *All Star Ken*, who not as macho as *Sport and Shave Ken*, lifted weights and had a flexible arm muscle.

The *International Barbies*, started in 1981 for collectors, added Eskimo and India to their growing numbers. These dolls are wonderfully made and destined to be quite valuable in the future. By 1987, there would be 14 in the series.

210. A special party was held for *Barbie* on Valentine's Day, 1984, in New York City, by invitation only. Souvenirs included a champagne glass and napkins printed for the occasion. *Crystal Barbie* and *Ken* enjoyed the ride in their *Silver Vette.*

211. *Loving You Barbie, Black Ken* and *Sweet Roses P.J.* attend the 25th celebration in the *Dream Carriage,* made just for the European market and one of the loveliest accessories ever made!

1983 was really a quiet year in our culture. There were lots of choices. *Angel Face Barbie*, who looked like sweetness and light, had cosmetics tied into Chesebrough-Ponds, Inc., and *Horse Lovin's Barbie, Ken and Skipper* kept the country idea alive with red "leather" jeans and "sheepskin" vests. *Skipper* got her own horse, *Honey*.

Hair was still popular, so another long hair doll appeared, *Twirly Curls Barbie*. Her beautiful long blonde hair could be styled with the help of a machine that twisted strands together. Another racial breakthrough came this year with an Hispanic version of *Twirly Curls Barbie*. The box showed an obviously Hispanic child playing with the doll; the entire box was in English-Spanish. No mention of her being Hispanic was on the box, again allowing *Barbie* to just be *Barbie* and not labeled. Available also was a black version. Now *Barbie* could truly be seen, like Santa Claus, as being whatever race a child wanted her to be. It was Ruth Handler's concept of a child projecting her identity on the doll at its best.

Dressing up was still important and *Dream Date Barbie* and *Ken* proved that with gorgeous satin-looking gowns and tuxedos. Most interesting was the *issue of Dream Date P.J.* in the same gown, but in another color. *Barbie* needed a friend to wear her clothes, but *Christie* was no longer used in this manner. The relationship of *P.J.* to *Barbie* had still yet to be explained.

Collectors eagerly awaited the arrival of two new friends for *Barbie* this year, *Tracy* and *Todd*, who were getting married. Most collectors were disappointed that *Tracy*, who used the *P.J.* face molds beautifully, had a sickly cast to her and washed out makeup as she was solely manufactured in the Phillipine factory. Even more disappointing was *Todd*, who was just *Ken*

212. 1985 saw more women in the work force than ever before. **Day to Night Barbie was an important woman executive, complete with attaché case and credit cards. Of course, in the evening, her look converted to glamour by reversing her outfit. Next to her is the rare Hispanic version sold in select areas. This was again a positive racial image enhancer. 213. The aerobic trend to fitness was shown by Great Shape Barbie, Ken and Skipper. Photograph courtesy Mattel, Inc.**

with different eye color. It was a shame an interesting concept could not have been more developed.

Finally in 1983, a gift set appeared that contained *Barbie, Ken* and *P.J.* in the same box. *Barbie* was very current in her "Valley Girl" mini and striped socks, but the real excitement was that the box announced that *P.J.* was *Barbie's Cousin*.

214. Oscar de la Renta fashions gave *Barbie* a couture look once again in 1985-86. High fashion magazines even carried the ads for these gowns such as the *Vogue* ad shown here. **215.** *Peaches 'n Cream Barbie* appealed to those more traditionally minded. She was also the first lead doll issued in another color besides *Barbie's* signature pink. *Photograph courtesy of Mattel, Inc.*

1984 was a big year in *Barbie* doll history. The company had decided to allow *Barbie* to be 25! In a hair color ad, Linda Evans of "Dynasty" fame proudly announced that "40 isn't fatal," and Joan Collins was a perfect size 8 at 50 years old. The baby boomers were forcing society to grow along with them. They simply refused to give up the crown. The term "Superwoman" came into being, to recognize a woman who at 35 looked perfect through diet, cosmetics and exercise, and also juggled the perfect job, the perfect child and the perfect house, all without help. Glamour and glitter were at a real high. Posh new clubs were opening again, featuring music carefully called "dance" music, which was the old disco beat, jazzed up with synthesized sounds.

In 1984, on Valentine's Day in New York, Mattel sponsored a party honoring the 25th birthday of *Barbie*. I personally attended this party and was very surprised at all the hoopla for this event.

Selected collectors had been invited, along with Mayor Koch of NY's office, and the press. The Gallery was decorated with the new *Loving You Barbie*, which just happened to be dressed in white with red velvet hearts all over her dress. Tiffany silversmiths had created a statue in sterling silver of a *Superstar Barbie* that was valued at $50,000 and would be touring the country. Mayor Koch's assistant announced that for the rest of the day, Fifth Avenue would be renamed "Barbie Boulevard." Everyone attending received nicely done champagne glasses and napkins with "Barbie's 25th Anniversary" on them. Mattel did not care if children thought *Barbie* was 25. With so many top models like Cheryl Tiegs, Catherine Deneuve and Jaclyn Smith hitting 40, there seemed little to fear from being 25. How different this thinking had become in just four short years!

Other exciting dolls that year were *Great Shape Barbie, Ken* and *Skipper*, who showed interest in another craze of the 1980s, AEROBICS. Developed to improve cardiovascular fitness, health clubs were springing up all over the country, as people of all ages did exercises to "dance" music. It was the next movement of the roller disco fad. After one got that great body, of course, it was necessary to show it off in gowns like *Crystal Barbie* owned.

Also very worthy of mention was *Sweet Roses P.J.*, and in my opinion, the loveliest *P.J.* ever. Her gown was made like fitted rose petals, and she was scented like a rose, also. No mention of her being *Barbie's* cousin was on the box, however. *Barbie* also got a new horse, *Prancer*, who was white, (really just *Dallas*, but another color) and a little pony named *Dixie*.

Started this year was a very lovely Collectors Series of fashions, the first of which featured a holiday outfit in red velveteen, (actually available the year before for Christmas), and included a springtime ensemble and a special silver dress and cape called *Silver Sensation* which was the official 25th birthday dress. A new policy was evolving where several of next year's dolls are shown immediately after Christmas as sort of a "sneak preview" of the new line and to capture holiday money a child may have been given. In the Philadelphia area, these dolls are on the shelves the week before Christmas as well!

By 1985, the woman's movement had come full circle. Finally being a woman executive was socially acceptable. *Barbie* again, set the pace by going from a busy executive with a gold credit card, to a night on the town in *Day to Night Barbie*. Her lovely day suit and spectator pumps give way to a chic cocktail dress for night wear. Not left out were black and Hispanic *Day to Night Barbie*, as well, making another positive statement about black and Hispanic women. The Hispanic version was only sold in selected areas and will

be a great collectible in the future. Also new was *Barbie's Home and Office*, where *Barbie* could work and play.

Fashion wise, the "designer" look in American culture was never hotter. Those in the fashion world knew that a "name" on anything from sunglasses to boxer shorts meant instant sales. For 1985, Oscar de la Renta "designed" a set of four stunning gowns, very "Dynasty" inspired. Those on the inside knew that a designer at Mattel had actually made the fashions, and Oscar just approved or disapproved them. This was standard practice with all designers.

Vogue magazine ran a two-page ad showing *Barbie* dolls with clever hairstyles modeling the gowns. Even the

216. In Philadelphia, Toys Я Us had exclusive rights to these two gift sets. 1986 *Vacation Sensation* on the left, and 1985 *Dance Sensation*. 217. A selection of the *International Barbies* from the Mattel catalog for 1987. This popular series shows *Barbie* can be from any culture or race.

218. "Dynasty," one of the most popular nighttime soaps, was synonomous with glamour. *Barbie* holds her own in a breathtaking Oscar de la Renta approved gown.

219. *Tropical Barbie* and *Barbie's Island Friend, Miko,* a lovely Eurasian new friend for *Barbie,* enjoy chatting with *Tahiti, Barbie's* parrot.

lead doll of the year, *Peaches 'n Cream Barbie,* (who also came in black), broke tradition from "*Barbie*" pink" and wore a peach chiffon gown.

A fun doll was *Dreamtime Barbie* and her bear, *BB.* Girls wanted to know that *BB* stood for. The obvious answer...*Barbie's Bear!* Dressed in a sheer nighty and robe, she was lovely.

Skipper was carefully dressed in workout gear in a gift set called *Hot Stuff Skipper,* but Mattel was very careful not to take her over the line they had crossed once with *Superteen Skipper* and *Scott.*

1986 started out very calmly with the introduction of *Magic Moves Barbie* who could move her hands through her hair. *Dream Glow Barbie* and *Ken,* dressed in almost Cinderella style,

220. For 1987, *The Rockers* were all redesigned with new fashions and hairstyles. *Ken*, with a more mature face and rooted hair, joined the group!

221. *Jewel Secrets Skipper*, new friend *Whitney*, *Barbie* and *Ken* are the glamorous new lead dolls for 1987. *Whitney* has super long hair. *Barbie's* life continues on into the future!

carried romanticism to new heights. What made 1986 different, forever, was the introduction of *Barbie and The Rockers.*

Rock and roll by 1986 was becoming respectible, if not patriotic, and was losing, except with some religious fanatics, its link to the drug culture. Celebrities such as Cher, Tina Turner, Bruce Springsteen and Patti Labelle denounced drugs emphatically as "uncool." Songs that had charitable purposes such as "We are the World" (which netted millions for starving worldwide), united singers from all over the world, giving rock music new respectability with parents and teachers. It did seem possible that one could

dress wildly and play loud music and still be a "decent" person. That is exactly what Mattel thought also because in a daring move, it was announced that *Barbie* would be the lead singer of a new group called, *The Rockers*. Announced in the *Barbie Drama* section of the *Barbie Magazine*, *Barbie* joined a group consisting of *Derek*, a Hispanic-looking boy, *Diva*, a redheaded all-American type, *Dana* an Oriental lovely and *Dee-Dee*, a black young lady. Portrayed as a struggling group with causes to conquer, they needed *Barbie* to lend her voice and support to the group.

222. 1986 was the 100th anniversary of Sears. To celebrate, Mattel issued *Celebration Barbie,* a fabulous doll in a pink ball gown. The collector of *Barbie* dolls should stock up on these specials, as they become instant collectibles when discontinued. This doll was available in retail outlets for only two months!

With the doll came a cassette tape of songs that told it all. Titles such as "Born with a Mike in My Hand," eased parents fears that *Barbie* had gone too far again. Of course, as a spokesperson for Mattel said, there were still traditional *Barbie* dolls and outfits, such as a wedding gown, available if one found this offensive. This, again, was just ONE of the many facets of *Barbie's* never ending skills. In fact, with the addition of the *Tropical* line of beach dolls, and *Barbie's* island friend, *Miko,* and parrot, *Tahiti,* it seemed there were plenty of personalities from which to choose in 1986!

If that was not enough, there were six more Oscar de la Renta gowns added to the Collectors Series, and more countries to the International Series. It certainly was true that *Barbie* could be whatever you wanted her to be. Unfortunately for the collector,

1986 was a banner year, but in terms of cash and space, a hard year indeed! By the end of the year, many collectors, myself included, were hoping *Barbie* would settle down just a bit, or by 1990, every closet in the house would be for *Barbie*!

Also that year was a new porcelain *Barbie* that was the start of a collectors series of dolls. Modeled after the *Superstar Barbie* and dressed in contemporary clothes, it is a nice doll and will probably be valuable in the future, but to me it is not *Barbie*. Many collectors, myself included, think of *Barbie* as vinyl and playable. The series will be continued with the next offering being a ponytail doll in *Enchanted Evening*.

Finally, 1987 saw a great new head mold for *Ken* that made him more "mature," to keep up with *Barbie's* timeless look. *Ken* also joined *The Rockers*, (probably to protect *Barbie* from *Derek*!). This year also saw the introduction of *Whitney*, a new friend with long dark hair for *Barbie*. The name, borrowed from popular singer Whitney Houston, is a highly visible name. The *Jewel Secrets* dolls, which includes *Whitney*, with clever stories, are also new for 1987.

1988 was a banner year at Mattel. At last the company was recognizing that a portion of their market was the adult doll collector. Prices and quality were creeping up. A special doll was issued for Christmas 1988 that had the doll world wondering what she would look like. The results were spectacular! The doll caused such a sensation that people waited in line like they did when the *Cabbage Patch Kid* dolls came out in 1983.

Even today, the 1988 *Happy Holiday Barbie* commands upwards of $200 mint in the package. It was a real message to Mattel that the collectors were eager for quality products.

223. The big news for 1986 was that *Barbie* had joined a rock group called, "The Rockers." Fashions were evolving again towards "Mod," but mixed with trash and flash! Not for every child, this *Barbie* was incredibly well received. "The Rockers" are: *Dana*, a charming Oriental, *Diva*, a devilish redhead, *Dee Dee*, a black pop star and *Derek*, a Hispanic-looking boy.

224. The Mattel catalog shows a new department store special doll for 1987, designed by Billy Boy, a New Yorker now in Paris, and called, *Feelin' Groovy Barbie*. The prudent collector will always add new and unusual versions of *Barbie* to his/her collection.

225. *Happy Holiday Barbie,* 1988 was the first "collector" doll. The price has more than doubled, twice, since the issue!

Other events of the year were "store specials." This would be a path that Mattel and the Alexander doll company would follow from this point on. A doll would be made-up, coiffed, dressed, and packaged especially for stores like Hills, Wal-Mart, F.A.O. Schwarz, and even the supermarket chain, Winn-Dixie! These dolls would be bought by collectors who were fortunate enough to live near one of these stores, then resold, usually at twice retail, to those who lived outside the area. Gradually over the years, various stores you would never dream of such as Ames, Sears, Spiegel, Child World, and K-Mart, as well as wholesale clubs would all have special dolls that would keep the collector hopping just to know what was available!

Regular line dolls for 1988 were *Perfume Pretty Barbie,* (available in both black and white), and *Barbie's* friend, *Whitney.* The dolls came with *Barbie's*

own fragrance and scented fashions.

One of the more interesting doll lines of the year was *Barbie and the Sensations.* Dressed like 1950s "do-wop" singers, the dolls sported a 1980s version of the 1950s. Loosely based on the Michael J. Fox movie, *Back to the Future,* where he went back in time to the 1950s, the dolls were dressed in spectacular clothing.

The beach theme was still popular this year with the addition of *Island Fun Barbie* and her friends. Dressed like they were marooned on an island, the whole gang came with grass skirts, and a "Swiss Family Robinson" hut to live in!

"*Barbie* bashing," or saying that the doll was just an empty-headed clothes horse was becoming popular in the media, as the economy dipped. To offset these charges, Mattel heavily promoted *Doctor Barbie, Doctor Ken,* and *Nurse Whitney.* Naturally, glamour could not be TOTALLY forgotten, for their costumes changed into glittery night wear when off duty!

The BIG news of 1988 was the reintroduction of *Barbie's Best Friend, Midge.* Absent since 1967, *Midge* was back, and with the *California Barbie* line, mothers and collectors went crazy with nostalgia, remembering the adventures that *Barbie* and *Midge* shared in the 1960s.

Also notable was that *Christie, Barbie's* black friend, had a new head mold that was very ethnic, and was highly acclaimed in the press.

All in all, 1988 was a tremendous year with many advances for *Barbie.* The porcelain dolls and the international dolls, as well as the store specials and the holiday doll, were propelling *Barbie* into mainstream collecting. It was a year to remember.

1989...Thirty Magical Years! Hard to believe, but this was the year an American legend celebrated her 30th anniversary as America's most popular doll. The *Barbie* doll was now bringing in close to

226. *Barbie and The Sensations* was a singing group that had a 1950s flair with 1980s style!

$800 million dollars a year for Mattel worldwide! This incredible success was based on several things. First, Ruth Handler, one of the founders of Mattel, had the uncanny vision to predict which trends would last. Secondly, the doll and the clothing *and* the personality of *Barbie* lent themselves to becoming a tradition. Thirdly, and perhaps most importantly, the children who played with, no worshipped, the world of *Barbie*, were in turmoil. They were "a ship adrift," according to the women's magazines of the day. Stability was a missing factor in daily life. Women saw their children confronted with child abuse, incest, AIDS, and other social ills. Reaching back to their childhood, women viewed the lifestyle

that *Barbie* represented as a rock; a never-changing pattern upon which dreams were built. *Barbie* was a "constant," and never more was this brought home than at Lincoln Center in February, 1989.

The thirtieth anniversary of the *Barbie* doll brought the media out in droves. My home was invaded by public relations officials who took literally hundreds of photographs of my collection. I was asked to write articles on *Barbie* in magazines as diverse as Delta Airlines to weekly women's magazines. The ultimate event was "The Anniversary...30 Magical Years" held at Lincoln Center. Here celebrities and collectors met, and the official souvenir was the ultimate *Barbie* collectible. A special doll, dressed in silver, with rhine-

227. *Doctor Barbie* proudly answered press charges that *Barbie* had no socially redeeming qualities. With her salary, she could afford the clothes that she wore!

stone jewelry, and tied in pink satin ribbon was issued in a limited edition of 1,200 pieces. It would be the most famous doll in *Barbie* history. One, it was *the* anniversary doll, and two, it was not given to collectors, but to the press, who neither understood, nor appreciated it. Some dolls were meant to be held back for the annual collector's convention, but because of last minute "gate crashers," all the dolls were given to the press and their representatives. It was a glaring "faux pas," and one that has made some collectors reject the doll as the ultimate doll in *Barbie's* history.

Other notable dolls in *Barbie* history were, another *Happy Holiday Barbie*, this time dressed in white, and just as lovely as the past years. Mattel, conscious of the shortages, issued the doll in record numbers, so that the doll flooded the market. Speculators, buying dozens of the dolls, are, as of this writing, having trouble selling the doll for issue price. Mattel was getting smart to the "secondary market."

228. *Benefit Performance* was the porcelain collector's doll of 1988. Some collectors like these dolls as well as the originals. *(Timeless Creations publicity photo.)*

229. *Mardi Gras Barbie* was the first in the *American Beauties Collection. (Timeless Creations publicity photo.)*

Dolls issued in 1989 also included the first F.A.O. Schwarz special *Barbie*, a UNICEF doll, and *Barbie* in the Air Force! Yes, times were a 'changing, and *Barbie* was to be the spokesperson for many a "cause."

Regular line dolls included *Superstar Barbie and Ken*, who were glamorous movie stars complete with "Oscars™," and *Animal Lovin' Barbie* which was available with some startling additions. Stuffed animals such as *Ginger, the Giraffe*, and *Zizzi, the Zebra*, were available. Those in the know knew that Hasbro had already planned to have their gorgeous *Jem* doll visit a Raja in a video adventure. He would give her a "Rama Lama" (surely based on the 1950s song "Ra Ma La Ma Ding Dong"). Samples were made up for Hasbro reps to distribute. I am fortunate to own one of these llamas. "Doll Wars" is an amazing phenomena. But the most amazing thing about the *Animal Lovin'* series was that a black version of *Barbie* was made but NOT a black version of *Ken*. The box for the black version of *Barbie* showed a black *Barbie* standing next to a white *Ken*. It was incredible that the press did not have a field day with *that* picture.

230. For 1989, *Happy Holiday Barbie* was dressed in white. Overproduced, the doll has not risen much in value, but in beauty, she is superb! **231.** Mattel became aware of social causes in the late 1980s. Always careful not to be controversial, *Barbie* became involved in issues such as UNICEF, which was certainly all-American.

232. Mindful of the public's image of *Barbie*, Mattel offered *Barbie* in the Air Force. Originally intended to sell only at military bases, the popularity of the doll warranted Mattel offering the doll to speciality accounts. *(Timeless Creations publicity photo)*

233. *Jazzie, Barbie's Cousin* was issued in 1989. Mattel, fearful that Hasbro's *Maxie*, with her young teen-age lifestyle would threaten the sophisticated *Barbie*, had their own young teen-age doll.

Dolls that year included *Style Magic Barbie*, and friends, and the new out-of-scale *Skipper* and her new friend *Courtney*. These dolls were beautiful, but the size of the head did not match, in my opinion, the scale used for *Barbie*.

New this year also were *Dance Club Barbie* and her friends, which looked very "Boy George," and *Cool Times Barbie* and the gang which drove a '57 Chevy which had little boys clamoring for this car!

The decade closed out with Mattel and *Barbie* being the best selling company and doll of all time, in the opinion of *Barbie* doll collectors.

The 1980s will always be remembered as the decade in which the doll collector won the battle of recognition with the major manufacturers of dolls and saw the doll artist market expand, not only with Mattel, but with exciting new innovations in the doll collecting hobby.

For *Barbie*, it truly was "Thirty Magical Years."

234. 1989 was the Pink Jubilee or Thirtieth Anniversary of the *Barbie* doll. A special press party was held at Lincoln Center in New York City, in February, to commemorate this event. Only 1200 of this special doll were made. It is the ultimate collectible in the world of *Barbie*.

235. A privileged few were invited to The Pink Jubilee with this silver platter. None have ever been offered for sale on the collector's market.

236. *Barbie's Best Friend Midge* returns in 1988 after being absent from the line since 1967.

237. *Dance Magic Barbie* and *Ken* were sensational. Hot and cold water changed his hair color and her lip color. *Timeless Creations publicity photo.*

Bob Gantz

IX.
The
Nineties
and On

A new decade! Where did time go? Who would ever think that "mod" would go out, and then come back in?

Mattel launched the arriving decade with an all-out campaign to win the doll collector's heart. It was true that *Barbie* had never looked better. Theme selection, hair rooting, costume design, all took on the look of dolls that were twice the price or more.

1990 began at Toy Fair in New York with the debut of the ultimate *Barbie* accessory, *The Magical Mansion*. The old expression, "you would have had to have been there" could never be truer. Curtains folded back, and this unbelievable mansion that glittered and sparkled rolled out while music played. It was the ultimate fantasy come true! The reality was that it cost $399, and worth every dime, but the space, well, you can imagine!

The lead dolls of the year were *Dance Magic Barbie* and *Ken*. While gimmicky, they were clever in design. Water made the lips and hair change colors.

Perhaps the most controversial dolls were the *Wet 'N Wild* series. Newspapers in Philadelphia labeled them "scandalous," but none took the time to realize that the name was based on a chain of theme parks!

Skipper got a boyfriend, *Kevin*, and *Barbie* and *Ken* skated with the Ice Capades. The tie-in spilled over so much that, when an Ice Capades show opened, a skater, coiffed and dressed like *Barbie*, led the opening of the show. It was a wonderful promotion.

To keep current, *Barbie and The Beat* arrived, complete with glow-in-the-dark outfits that were befitting a rock star. *Midge* was now a part of most of *Barbie's* adventures, and molds were switched to a smaller mouth that more matched *Midge's* grin in the 1960s.

With the emphasis on athletics and physical fitness, a workout promotion was instituted. *Barbie and The All-Stars* featured outfits that could, naturally, be converted to fancy party clothes after the workout.

My First Barbie, always rather plain, became quite glamorous as she and *My First Ken* were issued as Princess and Prince in wonderful outfits.

Also in 1990, *Wedding Fantasy Barbie* was introduced in white, lacy packaging. Mattel had always had imaginative packaging, which is why their dolls are worth so much more in the box than out. *Wedding Fantasy Barbie* was expensive. Even the discount houses had her for $29.95,

238. *Ice Capades Barbie* and *Ken* represented the first commercial tie-in in many years. The Ice Capades was celebrating 50 Years On Ice. A model dressed as *Barbie* introduced each show.

but collectors already proved that they would pay more for better quality. Few knew on the outside, that this would be a ten-year promotion based on the fact that since 1959, *Barbie's* wedding gowns have been the best seller every year!

New, also, was *Flight Time Barbie and Ken. Barbie* was available in black and Hispanic versions as well, but *Ken* was not. Since *UNICEF Barbie*, most of the lead dolls of the year were issued in at least three races, sometimes in four.

1990 was also the year that *Western Fun Barbie, Ken,* and *Nia* (really just the

Oriental face) became western travelers. Designer Ralph Lauren was doing a huge promotion on Navajo prints and other Southwestern clothing, and the dolls eerily copied these designs. Also available was a wonderful dog, *Turquoise,* and a horse, *Sun Runner.* Mattel owned a company called Arco, and many times it was hard to determine which accessories came from which company. This will be even more frustrating to collectors in the future. Arco catalogs are difficult to obtain and it is hard to keep up with all of the various products since they manufacture obscure sets for different stores in different sections of the country. Many items are added after the catalog is printed, so the collector will have to be on the go to find what he/she desires.

Another lead doll was *Home Pretty Barbie.* She was exactly like *Sweet Roses Barbie* that was a Toys R Us exclusive, and there were some hard feelings, but both dolls were popular and were really designed to live in the *The Magical Mansion.*

Added to the porcelain collections was a reproduction of *Barbie, Solo in the Spotlight* with a blonde ponytail, and a reproduction of *Barbie* in *Sophisticated Lady.* This doll sported a wig that was similar to the rare side-part dolls in the mid-1960s.

The big news of the year was that designer Bob Mackie was asked to design a *Barbie* doll. Indeed he did, for in my opinion, this doll is just too beautiful to describe! The most expensive *Barbie* ever, it came with a lithograph of Bob Mackie's design and a fabulous display case with the old *Barbie* logo. The old logo was on a round, pedestal stand as well. Retailing for $120, it was the most expensive vinyl *Barbie* ever made. In my opinion, the doll was far superior to the porcelain dolls which were much more expensive. The doll was launched with a huge promotion at Lincoln Center in February, and Timeless Creations debuted the doll in their

239. *Western Fun Barbie, Ken, Sun Runner* and *Turquoise (Barbie's* dog) pose in the Rocky Mountains.

showroom.

F.A.O. Schwarz had a fantastic doll called *Winter Fantasy Barbie*, that was dressed in a copy of the red dresses on the cover of the movie box for *White Christmas*, only these outfits were in blue velveteen. For fun, I bought an extra doll and had an expert seamstress make me one in red!

There were also many store specials in 1990, but after awhile they all seemed the same. Some surprises were in store for collectors at the end of the year!

In some wholesale shopping clubs, a gorgeous doll called *Party Sensation Barbie* appeared in magnificent packaging. Rumors abounded as to who the doll really was made for since, supposedly, these clubs only buy merchandise in quantity to sell inexpensively. The truth would not be known until late in 1991, but the doll was made by Mattel as a special for these wholesale outlets. What surprised everyone was the quality.

Western Fun Barbie and Sun Runner Gift Set which featured the doll and the horse attractively packaged in the same box, was also in the wholesale outlets and a few select Toys R Us stores.

Happy Holiday Barbie was issued in a, not so popular, pink dress, and also came in a black version. Unlike the dolls from the previous year, they still can be found on sale today. All in all, it was a year to remember.

1991 Toy Fair was a palace of new products in February. The lead dolls were *Costume Ball Barbie* and *Ken*. They could dress up in such outfits as a mermaid and a pirate. *Hawaiian Fun Barbie* and her friends was the beach promotion of the year, and in this series was *Barbie's Cousin Jazzie*, not to be seen again that year. Her presence was not that important now that Hasbros' *Maxi* was canceled.

Mattel held a huge press party with very tight security that I was fortunately asked to attend. The guests of honor were the new *M C Hammer* and *Lights & Lace Barbie* dolls! M C Hammer, himself, was in attendance, and a model was playing *Barbie*. It was a gala event.

240. The *Bob Mackie Designer Series* of *Barbie* dolls will be the most collectible dolls since 1959! Shown is the gold doll, first issued in 1990. *Timeless Creations* publicity photo.

Perhaps the biggest and best news of the year was that *Allan, Ken's* buddy, not seen since the late 1960s, was back with a fabulous new head mold. Granted, he now spelled his name *Alan*, (someone did not do their homework), but he and *Midge* were getting married in a fantastic gift-set box that included little *Kelley, Barbie's Sister*, and *Todd, Ken's Little Brother*. This set will be one of the great collectibles of all time. A trousseau wardrobe was available for *Wedding Day Midge*, as well.

Skipper had her own boyfriend this year, *Kevin*, who had the same big-eyed look as she did, and wore hi-tops to hang out at the mall.

There were some dolls that were definitely very child oriented such as *Bathtime Barbie*.

Ski Fun Barbie and *Ken*, were on the slopes, and collectors scrambled to find *Ski Fun Midge*, that was only sold in Canada, but later, she was in the United States in a Toys R Us exclusive version!

Also new were *Benetton Barbie, Christie*, and *Marina* later changed to *Kira* in the United States. The dolls were stunning with layers of clothing in Benetton colors. They were a beautiful series of dolls. In a move that is hard to understand, *Benetton Ken* and *Teresa* were not released in the United States. *Teresa* was especially gorgeous.

Another surprise was the reissue of three discontinued *International Barbies, Scottish, Parisian*, and *Eskimo*. In my opinion, the new versions of *Eskimo Barbie*, and *Parisian Barbie* were better than the originals. The *Scottish Barbie*, again, in my opinion was not as pretty as the first. What value this will have on the older dolls remains to be seen.

A stunning entry in the 1991 line was *Happy Birthday Barbie* available in both black and white. Once again, the party-type packaging would make it hard to open the doll. She was just gorgeous!

Another favorite of mine was *All-American Barbie*, and her friends. As in the previous year, her horse, *Star Stepper*, was available at wholesale clubs with the two packaged together. Wholesale clubs also had *Jewel Jubilee Barbie* in a gorgeous package. Once again, there were store specials from such stores as Ames, Hills, Wal-Mart, and even Service Merchandise which introduced *Blue Rhapsody Barbie*. It was a rough year for collectors both in terms of money and space.

Desert Storm, the war in the Middle East, made for a difficult beginning to the

241. 1991 was the year that *Barbie's Best Friend Midge*, and *Ken's Buddy Alan* got married, at last!

year. *Navy Barbie* in both black and white versions came to help children join in this conflict in a non-threatening way.

The porcelain collection continued this year with a brunette ponytail *Gay Parisienne Barbie*. One notable "faux pas" was that 350 of these dolls were to be held back for a special doll event at Walt Disney World® in December. These dolls would have special blonde ponytails. They were mistakenly not pulled from the shipments, and some lucky dealers would wind up with them. At press time, some eager collectors were paying $1,000 for this rare item that could turn up anyplace.

The *Ken* doll celebrated its thirtieth birthday, and was issued in porcelain. The ads for the doll showed a real *Ken* doll, so when the doll arrived, it was a surprise to many that he was not the doll in the advertising. It was a wonderful idea to promote this anniversary.

Happy Holiday Barbie arrived at stores in September, and in my opinion, was the best ever. Dressed in green velvet, she had a sequin-trimmed bodice and accessories. Available in both black and white, some oddities were that the black doll had green eyes, and some of the white dolls had fantastic make-up, while others lacked the black eye liner and full, red lips. All of this makes for shopping fun and keeps the collector mighty busy!

Speaking of sequins, this year there

242. Bob Mackie introduced two great dolls in 1991. *Starlight Splendor* was a black doll and the white version was called *Platinum*. Mattel boasted that 5,000 sequins were used on each doll! *Timeless Creations publicity photo.*

were *two* Bob Mackie designed *Barbies*. One was white, had platinum hair, and a gown and coat that allegedly had over 5,000 sequins on it! The black doll, wearing sequins and feathers, also wore a dress similar to what Diana Ross had worn on *TCB* (Takin' Care of Business), a television show special in 1968. A similar outfit also was used on the Bob Mackie-designed *Cher* dress for the doll that Mego produced in the late 1970s. That type of

244. *Dolls of the World Collection* was a name change from *The International Collection*. These three dolls were reissues of dolls previously issued by Mattel. *Timeless Creations publicity photo.*

243. *Swan Lake Barbie* was the first in a series of musical ballerina dolls that revolved on music boxes with etched lucite cases. *Timeless Creations publicity photo.*

245. Desert Storm, the armed conflict that involved United States' forces in the Persian Gulf, was the perfect backdrop for the issue of *Navy Barbie* in both black and white versions.

246. The porcelain series of *Barbie* has been available for several years through Timeless Creations, the collectible doll division of Mattel. One of the best is the *Sophisticated Lady*, 1990, with a rare side-part hair style. *Timeless Creations publicity photo.*

dress sure was popular, and I guess black *Barbie* should be proud that Cher and Diana Ross wore a version of her dress!

It is not the goal of this book to cover every doll and outfit. In actuality, many of the dolls and clothing are aimed at children, and it is doubtful that many would want everything for *Barbie* from every country. The commitment of both money and space would be overwhelming. Every year there are so many dolls and outfits, that I hope the reader will truly enjoy "the thrill of the hunt," and have many a fun day searching out elusive and interesting items for his/her collection.

See page 177 for more information.

X. Around The World With Barbie®

Just like children of each race and culture view Santa Claus as having their own characteristics, so it is with *Barbie!* One of the most rewarding and challenging parts of doll collecting is adding elusive European and other foreign items to your collection. Because of licensing agreements, these ethnically correct dolls are not available in the United States; many times, like in Japan, they are not even made by Mattel. The story of these items is indeed fascinating and a touch frustrating!

Lower airfares became a reality in the mid 1970s and opened up the entire world to many people. Some of those people just happened to be *Barbie* collectors!

One of the first "foreign" items to be found was *Barbie's Little Sister, Tutti,* a 6in (15cm) doll that had been available on the U.S. market from 1966 to 1971, but reportedly had been discontinued because of the new product safety codes. These well intended, yet severely abused codes, restricted manufacturers from making unique quality toys, and turned the responsibility for child safety over to them instead of where it belonged with the parent. As a result of these codes, a virtual "witch hunt" ensued, where U.S. agents actually went into toy stores and removed earrings from collector dolls such as Madame Alexander's. *Tutti,* her brother, *Todd,* and friend, *Chris,* were ruled unsafe because of the wire that was molded inside the dolls to make them posable. It was believed that if one was broken (or chewed) open, an injury could result.

Collectors traveling to England in 1973 were surprised to find *Tutti, Todd* and *Chris* still on the market, only dressed and packaged differently. Recently, it has come to light that *Barbie* was sold virtually in every country around the world starting with the "Bubble Cut" dolls in the early 1960s!

Another interesting fact is that the quality is much better for most foreign products. The accessories are more realistic, the clothing better made, and many times even the theme of the doll itself is more imaginative than a lot of the U.S. marketed items.

247. **Imagine! Who would ever think in 1959 that *Barbie* would be seen like this! *Rocker Barbie* from Rio de Janeiro, Brazil, 1986. Her quality is fantastic, with thick curly rooted purple afro and jointed wrists. Made under license by Estrella Company.**

Several reasons can be cited for this, the main one being that the rest of the world is really a two-class society, that of rich and poor, where the United States is made up a large middle class with about 20% of the population labeled as "rich or poor." In the U.S., Mattel aims *Barbie* mainly at this middle class, who for the most part view a toy as something you give a child to play with until it breaks, then replace it with something new. This is a relatively new attitude in this country, as "disposable" everything is a recent phenomenon. In most foreign countries, children are like they were here in the 1950s, whereby a child is given lovely things and taught to take care of them.

Also adding to this quality gap is that Americans consider their job a source of income to pay for their lifestyle, where in other countries, pride in one's work as a craftsman is still a means in itself. In all fairness, labor is cheap in some foreign countries and

248. 1976 *Gold Medal Barbie* from Australia. Issued worldwide for the Olympics, the design of her gold medal even included a kangaroo!

249. Mexico had wonderful gift sets! This 1981 set is titled *4 Estaciones* (4 seasons), and features a darker-skinned doll with four outfits.

this, too, widens the quality gulf for the collector.

In 1968, Elliot Handler stated that Mattel products were sold in over 60 countries. *Barbie* Fan Club members have been reported in such unlikely places as Zambia, Guam, Saudi Arabia, Cyprus, Turkey and New Zealand. The collector of these items would do well (and save much money) to make friends with airline personnel, for that seems to be the richest source of foreign *Barbie* items in the U.S.

The countries that produce the most interesting items seem to be those in which the American standard of beauty is idealized. In Japan, for example, the "preppie" look is still worshipped, and the Sandra Dee, Troy Donahue, blonde, blue-eyed standard is very much on a pedestal. Of course, like looking at a travel brochure of a city, these people have a media-induced view of American life that does not include crime, poverty or ghettos. What they see in news reports or in rock videos is what we WANT them to see, and like looking into a fishbowl, one does not view the entire ocean!

Many countries, like Australia, have pictured *Barbie* in pith helmet and safari gear. Ireland, long the land of shamrocks, has used green as the official color of *Great Shape Barbie,* depicted here in "aerobic teal blue."

Names are often changed of successful dolls to the resort of the particular country, as in *Malibu Barbie,* which is listed as *Saint Tropez Barbie* in French speaking countries and *Portofino Barbie* in Italian markets.

Health laws, again well intended but misdirected, also affect quality in European products. *Barbie's Horse, Dallas* and *Western Barbie* are real examples of the quality gap. The European version of *Dallas* is fully-jointed, like the *Dancer* horse of the early

250

251

250. The Estrella Company, now no longer a Mattel license, made some wonderful dolls in the 1980s. This doll, with top quality jointed wrists and many accessories, is called *The Beautiful One Who Is a Star.* 251. *Barbie 5th Anniversary Gift Set* from Spain. This gorgeous set from 1985 features a fabulous doll with dark skin and platinum hair. The quality of the doll is outstanding but the extra clothes are poorly made.

1970s made for the U.S. market. His mane is even real horse hair, which would be outlawed here. *Western Barbie* comes with an extra outfit and features jointed arms and the "busy" hands which open and close and were part of the early 1970s line. The dolls cost much more in these foreign markets (almost double), but are aimed at a higher audience than the American doll. To doll collectors, it is very reminiscent of Madame Alexander dolls here in this country which are directed at the upper class.

Particularly of note were the gorgeous dolls made by the Takara Company in Japan, under license from Mattel, which were unbelievably well

made. Photography in the catalogs rivaled the finest fashion magazines, and many times the lifelike quality of the dolls is uncanny. Modeled after the old "Speed Racer" cartoons, the dolls have big round eyes highlighted with three slash lines at the outer corners and silky blonde hair. The Oriental race must see our eyes as huge and round, for all the cartoons and dolls out of Japan have the same shape to the eyes.

The life-style of *Barbie* and *Ken* in Japan again depicts college life with the idealized standard of an outsider looking in at only what the "Chamber

252. Canada, right across our borders, has always been a rich source for unusual *Barbie* dolls. From left, *Hawaiian Superstar Barbie*, 1978; *Picture Pretty Barbie*, 1978; *Fabulous Fur Barbie*, 1985; and *Partytime Barbie*, available in two faces, 1977. 253. Mattel claimed that *Barbie* was not sold in Japan in the late 1970s, but this great gift set featuring a *Superstar Barbie* and her *Starcycle* was bought there in 1978!

of Commerce" wants you to see, and depicts *Barbie* much the same way as she was in the early 1960s here.

Recently a new company, Bandai, in Japan, received the Mattel license and combined with them to form "MA-BA" (Mattel-Bandai), to make new creations. Mattel seems interested in scaling down the creative aspects of *Barbie* as these new dolls lack the realism and imagination of the Takara dolls. Takara, on the other hand, continued using all their old ideas in a new doll called *Jenny* which is a collectible in itself, but is not at all tied into *Barbie*.

In France, a doll of a French country singer in the early 1980s joined the *Barbie* family, in the guise of *Chantal Goya*. The doll was billed as "being able to wear *Barbie's* lovely fashions," and followed the pattern started with *Julia* here in the U.S., where a licensed "friend," as it were, was able to share *Barbie's* bountiful wardrobe!

Canada has also been a source of *Barbie* dolls with creative themes.

Hawaiian Superstar Barbie used the Superstar molds in ethnic fashion before the U.S. did, and each year the Canadian market gets a "set" of *Barbie* and *Ken* with a theme, such as 1987s *Tennis Barbie* and *Tennis Ken*. The strange thing is that almost without fail, the accompanying *Skipper* doll that matches the set, and is even shown on the box, is not sold in Canada, but is available only in England, France, Italy and Germany! No explanation for this is ever given, and has frustrated many a collector when visiting Canada to buy the latest *Barbie* dolls.

255. Booklet from Japan, 1969, showing *Barbie's* friend, *Living Eli*. This is the rarest of all the *Barbie* friends. Interestingly, her face mold showed up in the U.S. on a cheaply made doll Mattel made for discount stores called *Sweet 16*.

254. The pride and joy of any *Barbie* collection are the foreign items that show *Barbie* as she appears to that culture. This very rare *Hundslade* (hound sled), was offered in 1981 for the Scandanavian countries. The doll is the beautiful *Snoprinsessa Barbie* (Snow Princess Barbie) that pictures *Barbie* in the land of the midnight sun.

256

257

258

259

256. One of the most beautiful sets ever made for *Barbie* was this *Equestrienne Barbie and Her Horse, Dancer,* sold in Canada, 1977. The doll was the old *Barbie* face with rooted eyelashes, not seen in years in the U.S., and *Dancer* was fully-jointed.

257. American native Billy Boy persuaded Mattel, France, to make this edition of *Barbie* in 1985. Billy Boy sees *Barbie* here as his "dream girl," and dresses her as such. This doll was part of a display that toured the U.S. featuring designer gowns for *Barbie.*

258. Germany has long been a source of great *Barbie* treasures. 1986 saw these great *Music Lovin' Barbie, Ken* and *Skipper* offered for sale. As usual, the *Ken* and *Barbie* were available in Canada, but not the *Skipper!* No explanation of this has been found!

259. The Takara Company of Japan had the most famous license in Mattel history. Producing dolls that were perfect miniatures of American life, they did their job so well, they threatened domestic sales as so many dolls were imported illegally. They lost their license in 1986. This set of *Barbie* and *Ken* show American teenagers as seen through the eyes of the Japanese.

Also of note is that *Ken* is often dressed in outfits that here would draw stares as being too "high fashion" for middle class American men not as style conscious as their European counterparts.

Other interesting comments on foreign *Barbie* items include the mention that all Mexican dolls are darker skinned, with "bleached" looking blonde hair. More noteworthy, however, is the fact that so many of the Mexican dolls were being brought across the border by doll dealers to sell here, that the government made the factory shrink wrap ALL *Barbie* dolls to prevent drug smuggling in the doll boxes!

In Spain, again *Barbie* is made with darker skin but has incredibly fine, platinum blonde hair that seems not to match her skin tones, but implies "dye job," or "movie star hair." The quality of the doll made for Spain is again better than the U.S. dolls, but the clothing quality is not as nice.

In the late 1980s, Mattel and Bandai parted ways as a joint effort, and Bandai took over the manufacture of *Barbie* in Japan. The dolls were original, "cute," but by now, the Japanese girls knew about and wanted the real thing...the American *Barbie*. The arrival of Toys R Us in Japan also marks the arrival of *Barbie* just as she is sold here.

One interesting note; Takara continued making the very same doll that had represented *Barbie*. They now call her *Jenny*. Recently, in a newsletter to little Japanese girls, Takara said that *Jenny* was celebrating her tenth anniversary. The reason? For five years, *Jenny* dreamed she was *Barbie*! Thus providing endings like those on *Dallas* and *Twin Peaks*!" This is what makes fashion doll collecting so exciting!

260. The "swan song" of Takara was this *Mink Barbie*, featuring *Barbie* in a designer dress and real ranch mink coat. The styling of the case and the stand were first class. It is sad that dolls like this are not offered on the U.S. market!

261. In 1986, Mattel combined forces with a Japanese company, Bandai, to form MA-BA. Mattel wanted closer control over the Japanese products. The MA-BA *Barbie* and *Ken* are nice, but lack the imagination of the Takara dolls. Takara has recently won a lawsuit against the Bandai company for using their basic mold ideas.

One should mention also that almost all Mattel dolls are currently made either in the Phillipines, Taiwan, Malaysia or Hong Kong. The Phillipines manufactured dolls appear first in the stores and are not the quality of those made by the other factories. Often they are "orange" in skin tone, with pale, washed out makeup. On the lead doll for 1987, *Jewel Secrets Barbie*, even those manufacturered for the European markets had a sickly orange cast to them with little makeup.

Brazil was just recently one of the best places to buy unique, different *Barbie* dolls, made under license by the Estrella Company, but collectors traveling there in February 1987, were told that the company had surrendered their license. Their ideas were wonderful, and often used old molds they must have obtained from Mattel at some point, as packaged with the dolls were items not sold here in years, such as little curling irons and barrettes.

262. *Barbie* by the Takara Company in Japan was seen as having big eyes and blonde hair. She came dressed in the traditional kimono, and as *Romantic Barbie* on the right.

263. The richness of the Takara gift sets was like something made here in the 1950s. Fabulous satin dresses, fur coats and minute accessories made *Barbie* come alive. This set made for Christmas 1985, featured *Barbie* photographs that were like studio portraits! Lucky is the collector who has these sets!

264. Designer tie-ins for the Takara *Barbie* like this coordinating set made by Kansai, rivaled Bloomingdale's displays! This set is light years ahead of the American *Barbie* fashions.

The Scandinavian countries also have produced some great items such as *Snow Princess Barbie*, depicting *Barbie* with the fine dark hair and pale skin of those not exposed to harsh sunlight further south.

It is safe to say that the collector of *Barbie* dolls can assemble a veritable smorgasbord of dolls from around the world that represent *Barbie* with almost every racial feature imaginable. This is as it should be, and a sign that we are moving into some enlightenment, at least, where people are satisfied with who and what they are, rather than wishing to be some idealized standard. By viewing a strong, independent character such as *Barbie*, who CAN do anything, and really has been successful, (and is their own race), a child strengthens his/her own self-esteem. Through playing with a *Barbie* doll that represents that child's race, egos are enhanced and even relations with the U.S. improve. For too long Americans have had a negative image abroad and now that situation is being helped by, of all things, *Barbie!*

Truly, the collector of *Barbie* dolls around the world cannot help broaden his/her perspective as well, and learn to appreciate ALL cultures worldwide. For the collector who likes to specialize, these elusive foreign dolls make a challenging hobby, and one that adds to peace and contentment in world relations. A trip around the world with *Barbie* is indeed a wise investment!

265. In 1986, Takara borrowed the original ponytail molds from Mattel and produced these fantastic dolls, dressed by designer Hiomichi Nakano. Simply called *American Doll*, they were as well made as the American dolls of the 1960s.

266. PB, a department store in Japan, convinced Mattel and Bandai to reissue the old faces from the 1960s. These outstanding dolls are made from the old ponytail, bubble cut, and twist and turn faces. The clothing is either reproductions of older outfits, or as shown here, original designs. The logo shown is *Barbie* as was seen in the 1960s!

XI. Tammy®. The Doll You Love...To Dress

By 1961, the popularity of *Barbie* was well established. Every major and minor manufacturer had entered the teen fashion doll race. The truth was the market was so large AND so popular that there was room for all. The face of the doll market (and society) had changed much, from emphasis on the child, to catering to the teenage market; everyone was making money off the miniature teen fashion doll craze. The boom children refused to let go of the attention of the nation (a trait they still possess as today women over 40 dominate the fashion and entertainment field).

Some executives of toy companies and parents still felt in 1961 that *Barbie* was too sexy and "over-developed." Also, the baby boom had lasted so long that there still were hoards of younger children coming up. Like waves on the ocean, these children, now in elementary school, kept filling up the homes and schools of America. Not having been raised on the Marilyn Monroe type of glamour, these pre-teens could perhaps be "soft peddled" slightly on the role sophistication would play in their lives.

The Ideal Toy Corp., long famous for making money off their child star dolls, felt now was the time to act. In 1962, they issued *Tammy, The Doll You Love...To Dress*. Not as old as *Barbie*, nor as shapely, *Tammy* seemed a bit less threatening to the values of the day. Minus, too, was the presence of a boyfriend. In fact, *Tammy* had a complete family that consisted in her height of popularity of *Mom, Dad,* brother *Ted*, little sister *Pepper, Dodi,* a friend of *Pepper's* and little brother *Pete*. Opposite to *Barbie*, *Tammy's* friends seemed to be "racier" than *Tammy* herself. Friend *Glamour Misty* wore silver glitter outfits that were far more sophisticated than *Tammy's* image; the *Miss Clairol Doll*, made from the same molds bleached her hair in shocking colors.

All in all, the glamous image that many moralists found offensive was missing in *Tammy*. Ideal specifically designed her to be 12in (30cm) tall so that she could not be in scale to *Barbie*. For the most part, the fashions between the two dolls were not interchangeable,

---

267. By 1964, *Tammy* had been allowed to grow up slightly. New *Posn' Tammy* sported an American Girl hairdo just like *Barbie* and wore couture inspired clothing.

268. *Tammy, The Doll You Love...To Dress,* dressed as Queen of the Prom. 269. Debbie Reynolds in her role as Tammy. Produced by Ross Hunter, the Tammy movies, starring Reynolds and Sandra Dee, tied in the down-to-earth image of the American family. *Movie Star News photograph.*

Tammy®, Picnic Party®, Beau and Arrow®, Sorority Sweetheart® and School Daze® are registered trademarks of the Ideal Toy Corp.

Clever outfits such as *Picnic Party* and *Beau and Arrow* were designed with amazing attention to detail. *Sorority Sweetheart* and *School Daze* all told the story of an ORDINARY girl's high school life. This was at the heart of the difference between *Tammy* and *Barbie.* *Tammy* was just an average schoolgirl like those of the TV sitcoms of the day. *Barbie* was a globe-trotting high fashion model that was so perfect that reality was stretched almost beyond the beliefs of many simple American children.

The three or four years separating this current 1962 generation of pre-teens and those ahead of them was surprisingly eventful. A movie producer, Ross Hunter, in the late 1950s believed that movies could capture once again the audience lost to television if only GLAMOUR was reintroduced. The gorgeous "women's pictures" of the 1930s, such as *The Women,* were indeed gone from the screen. With *Imitation of Life, Portrait in Black* and *Backstreet,* Hunter lured the "costume" effect back into fashion. Spawned during this period, *Barbie* mirrored the fantasy projection of a woman-child traveling the world of glamour. The next group of teens had missed out on this entirely and saw *Tammy* as a more down-to-earth role model. Even Mattel lessened *Barbie's* sophistication by 1964, when her careers centered more around her college days than her modeling talents.

meaning the owner of *Tammy* had to purchase a separate wardrobe. The same tie-in concept with other products was tried, however, as *Tammy* had storybooks, paper dolls, record albums and dozens of licensed products.

The clothing itself was stunning and just as well made as the *Barbie* fashions. Many *Barbie* collectors today consider themselves "traitors" to collect other fashion dolls, but like the macho man who has learned that sensitivity is a blessing, *Barbie* collectors are discovering other dolls that tell the fashion story as well as *Barbie.*

The other concept behind *Tammy* was one of the American family. *Barbie*

270. The less developed figure of *Tammy*, and her school girl image, made her one of the most popular teen fashion dolls ever. Storybooks were available of her down home adventures.

271. *Glamour Misty*, *Tammy's* racy friend, came in a phone booth. Her outfit, a silver lame jumpsuit, was a far cry from *Tammy's* earlier image. With her "flip" hairdo, she had much more personality than *Tammy* herself.

had been just three years too soon to benefit from the all-American image that the family had in the early 1960s. Shows like "Ozzie and Harriet," and the aforementioned "The Donna Reed Show" and "Father Knows Best," all portrayed a stereotyped image of the American family that even today is regarded by many to be the ideal. This type of family, perfect in every way, became almost a neurotic obsession for many of the period; a fantasy that has sent many a woman to the psychiatrist's couch trying to figure out how to dust curtain rods and bake cookies at the same time while still looking "crinoline crisp" with a string of pearls!

Tammy had come along at just the correct time. In 1963 Ideal issued dolls representing her father, called appropriately *Dad*, brother *Ted* (who shared the same Ivy League wardrobe), and, of course, *Mom*, whose outfits consisted mainly of housedresses to care for her family, and an occasional "evening gown" for that special yearly night out. In fact, that was the dilemma of the American teen by 1963. The life they led was so much fun, so chock full of activities and self-exploration that many would find "settling down" a prospect not to be considered until decades later.

As the popularity of *Tammy* increased, Mattel responded by "taming

down" *Barbie*. By the mid-1960s, both dolls sported "American Girl" hairdos and wore couture clothes. It was this "equality" that spelled the end for the *Tammy* saga. Mattel was known for its uncanny ability to predict which direction society was moving (a trait they still possess today). *Barbie* was outselling *Tammy* drastically. The final "blow" came when the British Invasion occurred in 1965. Ideal was simply not geared financially to redesign the *Tammy* "All American" concept as Mattel did with *Barbie*. Suddenly American teens no longer looked to their own country for their image. Like a clock ticking backwards 200 years, England and the Beatles took "the colonies" by storm. *Tammy* died a graceful death, like Mary Stone on "The Donna Reed Show." *Barbie*, MODified and updated, moved on. The race was over and *Barbie* had won. The collector of teen fashion dolls was really the winner, for today, *Tammy*, *The Doll You Love...To Dress*, is now a doll you love to collect!

Tammy®, *Glamour Misty*®, *Dad*®, *Ted*® and *Mom*® are registered trademarks of the Ideal Toy Corp.

158

XII. Tressy® And Judy Littlechap®...

In 1963, more contenders entered the lucrative teen fashion doll race. By this time, *Barbie* was selling at the rate of over six million dolls a year! Mattel was the largest manufacturer of ladies clothing in the world; it just was doll size. The arrival of *Fashion Queen Barbie* with her three wigs began a few years of hair play emphasis. One doll that entered the race rose to the place of real competition. Her name was *Tressy*.

The American Character Doll Co. was no stranger to fashion dolls. Having secured the *Toni* license from The Gillette Company when Ideal tired of it, this firm issued gorgeous high heel fashion dolls bearing the *Toni* name. It is interesting to note how the *Toni* doll had grown along with the boom children, from a toddler image of the present, to the future image of sophistication. The company also issued the same doll as *Sweet Sue Sophisticate*. Equipped with a bra and nylons, she came in the demure size of 10in (25cm) and definitely was a forerunner of *Barbie*.

Tressy had a magic feature that both *Tammy* and *Barbie* lacked. Her hair "grew!" A long strand of hair could be pulled out of the top of her head. A brass key in the shape of a "T" was inserted in her back to rewind the "secret strand," as it was called. The rest of *Tressy's* hair was one length to her chin. The styling possibilities were endless. American Character, known for their quality dolls, had a winner. Her fashions, however, left much to be desired, but American Character dolls were not known for their clothing, but for their rich, heavy vinyl.

Like the other fashion dolls, *Tressy* was available in a wide range of hair colors. The missing element in her story, however, was any kind of personality. *Tressy* was just another teenage girl who was pretty and had lots of wonderful clothes. Actually, she cost $4.98 in 1963, which was more than the other fashion dolls did, but the growing hair feature warranted this higher price.

272. American Character's *Tressy®* sports a 1960s "Beehive" hairstyle. Included with the doll was a fashion booklet, shown right. The *Tressy's Hair Glamour* book, published by Dell, showed all *Tressy's®* hairstyle fashions.

By 1965, *Tressy* had gained a little sister, *Cricket*, who also had the grow hair feature and a "best friend," *Mary Make-Up*. Like with all fashion dolls, the term "best friend" implied that both dolls were the same size and able to share clothing.

Collectors of teen fashion dolls often overlook the *Tressy* wardrobe, mainly because it is so difficult to find mint-in-box. These outfits are very unique, with themes that add so much to the study of 1960s pop culture. Outfits such as *Hooray! Hootenanny Tonight* told of the country singing so popular in 1963, and *Party of the Year!*, where *Tressy* becomes "Miss American Character," giving her real status as a winner. Because these outfits were not as plentiful as *Tammy's* or *Barbie's*, they are very difficult to find today. A complete MIB collection of them is quite rare and if the demand were higher, would command much more than *Barbie* clothing would.

The hair play aspect of *Tressy* became so popular that in 1965, Dell Publishers made a little "pocket book" of hairstyles that could be done for *Tressy*. Folks may fondly remember the little Dell books that were available in the checkout line at the supermarket on subjects that ranged from diets to dog care. *Tressy's Hair Glamour* was such a publication and is a real period piece to fans of hairstyles. Complete instructions were given to construct such enduring styles as "Beach Beauty Bob," a sleek pageboy, or "World's Fairest Do," a flip with top braid to wear to the New York World's Fair! Other teen dream styles included "Royal Pouf," a jeweled upsweep, and, of course, a "Beehive Bubble" to wear to a "pink champagne ball."

Tressy was what today psychologists call a "conspicuous consumer," for she definitely reveled in the status symbols of the day. No visible means of support was offered for her life-style, and in my opinion, this was really the missing element that led to her demise.

In 1965, *Mary Make-Up*, *Tressy* and *Cricket* all came in gift sets with hair color or hair play accessories. *Tressy* also had her own apartment "for gracious living," which led the more astute child to wonder just who "kept" *Tressy* in the life-style to which she had become accustomed. Her age seemed a mystery as well, but few 16-year-olds could be living on their own in a penthouse. This year was the last year *Tressy* and her world were offered. 1966 showed no listing for these dolls in most catalogs.

Perhaps *Tressy's* family or whomever had gotten tired of supporting her...maybe she married and left town, but for whatever reason, *Tressy* was gone. The collector of this doll has a real job to do, for *Tressy*, her friends and her fashions are the most difficult to find of all the teen fashion dolls. Fortunate is the collector who has been foresighted enough to collect these dolls. I predict that *Tressy* has a great future as a collectible!

273. The *Littlechap Family* by Remco Industries idealized the upper class American family. Daughter *Judy* was the "wealthiest" of all the fashion doll princesses!

Tressy®, Cricket®, Mary Make-Up®, Hooray! Hootenanny Tonight® and Party of the Year® are all registered trademarks of the American Character Doll Co.
Tammy® is a registered trademark of the Ideal Toy Corp.

Naturally, the *Barbie* doll story must be the longest tale of the fashion doll saga because of *Barbie's* 30 years of existence. Other dolls of one or two years duration can tell us just as much about the slice of life they represent.

Judy Littlechap is such a doll. The largest of the teen fashion dolls, 13½in (35cm), her story is also the grandest. Remco Industries was a stranger to the doll business. They were best known for boys' toys with an action theme. Perhaps this is why they could enter the fashion doll race with, in my opinion, the most imaginative of all the teen fashion dolls.

On the drawing boards in 1962, the *Littlechap Family* did not make its appearance into the toy stores until 1964. The family made no apologies about being upper class. The slice of life they offered was one of perfection and stability. The father of the family, *Dr. John Littlechap*, was described as having "a masculine movie star physique, graying at the temples." His accomplishments in the booklet that accompanied all the dolls and outfits listed him as "a member of the Lanesville County Medical Society, former Flight Surgeon U.S. Army Air Force... and loves his family and golf."

Naturally anyone that wonderful would have an equally outstanding wife. *Lisa Littlechap*, elegantly coiffed in a "beehive" that had streaks of gray, was "a former model, wonderful cook...president of the P.T.A., and the best dressed woman in town."

Their two daughters were, naturally, highly motivated and the kind of daughters one would expect a doctor and his wife to have. *Libby Littlechap*, kid sister of the family was, "age 10, fifth grader at Lanesville Elementary School...loves to climb trees, pester her sister, and wants to be a doctor like her daddy." (Of course, this was only a hero worship dream, as her destiny more than likely would be changing drapes in her gorgeous home than changing uniforms).

The eldest daughter, *Judy Littlechap*, was the "big sister" of the *Littlechap Family*. Described as "age 17, honor student at Lanesville High, she loved parties and crazy desserts." Two kinds of children seemed to enjoy playing with the *Littlechap Family*---those who lived the very life they represented and those who wished they did. Children are, in my opinion, much more astute than adults give them credit for, and many a little girl saw herself in *Judy Littlechap*, or the self that she longed to be. Whatever the reason, *Judy Littlechap* was a quality doll with an uncanny resemblance to Jacqueline Kennedy. Many novice doll collectors often think that the *Judy Littlechap* doll is a portrait doll of Mrs. Kennedy. Indeed, the message of grace and class is the same. The *Littlechaps* behaved "correctly," and were the epitome of the upstanding family of the time.

The collector of these dolls does not have too difficult a time amassing a

---

274. Judy Littlechap® **wears Judy's Football Outfit**®**, 1964. Naturally, a well bred young lady like Judy would attend all the "right" games and, of course, wore Princeton colors and a mum, as was the custom.**

Judy Littlechap® *Littlechap Family*®, *Dr. John Littlechap*®, *Lisa Littlechap*® and *Libby Littlechap*® are all registered trademarks of Remco Industries.

mint-in-box collection. The dolls did not sell well and much old store stock has remained. When researching this section of the book, this author was able quite easily to obtain every outfit ever made for *Judy Littlechap* mint in the box within a period of 30 days. This availablility gives a false impression, however, that interest or quality is lacking. Fashion doll collectors are turning to the other dolls from the past 30 years that represent the history of fashion and pop culture. These outfits will soon disappear into the collections of the astute collector, raising the prices on them to the level they should be for something so nice that is from 1964.

My theory of why the dolls were not a success is based on several facts. It is only today, when we look backward at the dolls and their outfits, that we see the brilliant social statement they make. Our quest for "nostalgia" (which is to me a longing to have again something you took for granted at the time) plus our added knowledge about sociology and even fashion, make the owner of the *Littlechap Family* wish life could again be that simple. What did *Judy Littlechap* know of poverty, crime or despair? Her life as the daughter of a wealthy doctor shielded her from contact with any of life's unpleasantnesses. Collectors today are desirous of all these statements the doll makes.

In 1964, however, who knew that the assassinations of leaders, the Vietnam War and the drug culture lay just ahead to disturb the peace! The *Littlechaps* must be viewed with 1960s eyes to make a critical judgment. The truth is that the dolls were AWKWARD. Limbs were too long, feet turned out at angles, faces devoid of character...all

these led to the rapid demise of this family of dolls.

Today, older and wiser, the *Littlechap Family* is remembered more for what it says about our ideas of perfection in 1964 than our standards of workmanship. The psychological and sociological message of many modern dolls is the REAL appeal to most collectors. Those who do not feel this often find the attraction to these dolls strange as they are judging them on quality alone. To those who collect them, teen fashion dolls are a three-dimensional textbook of America as we would like to remember it.

OPPOSITE PAGE: The upper class family known as the *Littlechaps*, here described ever so "properly" on the back of their wardrobe boxes.

Judy Littlechap® and *Littlechap Family*® are registered trademarks of Remco Industries.

The *Littlechap* Family

Meet the Littlechap family: Dr. John Littlechap; Lisa, his wife; their two daughters — 17 year old Judith and 10 year old Libby.

Never before has a family of dolls been created that is so true to life. Be sure to see and buy them at your favorite toy store.

Judith Littlechap

friends call her Judy — age 17 — honor student at Lanesville High School — Senior class — loves parties and crazy desserts.

Libby Littlechap

age 10 — fifth grader at Lanesville Elementary School — loves to climb trees, pester her sister, and wants to be a doctor like her Daddy.

Lisa Littlechap

attractive mother of Judith and Libby — former model — wonderful cook — President of the P.T.A., and best-dressed woman in town.

Dr. John Littlechap

member of the Lanesville County Medical Society — former flight surgeon U. S. Army Air Force — loves his family and golf — wishes he could find more time for both.

REMCO INDUSTRIES, INC.   JAPAN

275. Kenner's *Darci*® was the outstanding fashion doll of the late 1970s.

Darci® is a registered trademark of Kenner.

XIII. Et Al...

It would be an impossible goal to list all the teen fashion dolls of the past 30 years. Even more impossible would it be to illustrate all the thousands of fashions made for them. This genre of doll, born really in the late 1950s, is still the mainstay of the doll industry. Dolls have come and gone, some so generic and cheaply made that they are not worthy of mention. Others have been wonderful, and quite frankly overlooked by teen fashion doll collectors. Any successful product is going to be copied. Imitation is the sincerest form of flattery. Like *Barbie* took the teen fashion dolls of the 1950s one step further, some other dolls since 1959 also have made brilliant statements of our culture.

Unfortunately for the doll collector, money was usually the motivator behind the release of any doll. A company is in business to show a profit. Usually there are stockholders to answer to, bills to be paid; the more popular dolls produce more money. As any viewer of television who has had a favorite series canceled can tell you, the most popular is not always the best! Like Nielsen ratings determine which shows get the ax, so do financial reports determine which dolls remain and which ones are discontinued.

This is why the fashion doll collector would do well to add currently available dolls to their collections that appeal to them when they see them. When sales dip, or never take off, these items rapidly disappear. If a company declares bankruptcy, inventory is sometimes taken right off the shelves! Just like a television viewer would be wise to tape a treasured program lest it never be seen again, so should the doll collector buy on sight those items which appeal to them. The words "popular," and "esthetic" are NOT the same, and many good dolls such as Kenner's *Darci* were of unbelievable quality, but for some reason did not appeal to the masses. Also, when collecting play dolls that are in reality designed for young children (the age of playing with dolls is lower than it was in 1959), what is attractive to you as an adult collector might be above the level necessary for the doll to succeed as a child's toy.

Sometimes the opposite spells the demise of a doll. Even the prestigious Alexander Doll Co., Inc., felt obligated to enter the teen fashion doll race. In fact, so committed were they that their entry, *Brenda Starr*, was the "cover girl" on their 1964 catalog. Advertised

in the catalog (Alexander dolls were never on television, much too vulgar a medium) as "different from any other doll of this type, of a finely finished high grade of plastic," the doll also featured sleep eyes and a rooted non-retractable long strand of hair like *Tressy's*. Naturally what made *Brenda Starr* worthy of competing was that her fashions were made with the Alexander magic touch of high quality.

The company hoped that mothers and daughters, seeing the obvious high quality of *Brenda Starr*, sold only in "better" stores, would buy her instead of *Barbie*. They were wrong. The age of the wealthy child living in a vacuum was over, thanks to television, and TV was where *Barbie* was making it big. Despite the fact that *Brenda Starr* WAS the high quality doll she claimed to be, and even though she came in exquisitely packaged gift sets, little girls were mesmerized by *Barbie* in 1964, much the same way children were by *Cabbage Patch Kids* dolls in 1983.

Finally in 1965, deciding probably that paying extra for the *Brenda Starr* license was making no difference in sales, Alexander issued the exact same doll and called her *Yolanda*. Available only in 1965, *Yolanda* is fantastic and another doll that is often overlooked by teen fashion doll collectors. Offered as a bride, she was stunning. Also issued was a heavy satin formal with sequin-trimmed bodice and a gorgeous

276. *Brenda Starr*® was Madame Alexander's entry into the fashion doll contest in 1964. A lovely high quality doll, she did not catch on with the public. 277. Kenner issued *Dusty*® in 1974. Overly athletic and not very feminine, she was rapidly discontinued.

pleated tulle formal with roses in her hair.

The obvious answer to why a doll is discontinued is because it is not selling well. *Brenda Starr* and *Yolanda* will be remembered as the "rich man's *Barbie*." Even today, when most Alexander dolls from that period are bringing fantastic sums when mint, these dolls have not risen in value like others have. The dolls, like a wonderful TV movie, disappeared, never to be seen again.

Doll companies were having so much trouble competing with *Barbie* that most major manufacturers just gave up. For the rest of the 1960s, and on into the early 1970s, there was not a serious challenger for a piece of the fashion doll pie. Naturally, at the supermarket or drug store one could still see in plastic bags the blank-faced cheaply made teen fashion doll imitators, but a real doll with an image, a name and a personality was simply not worth the trouble.

Finally in the early 1970s, a breakthrough occurred. As discussed in a previous chapter, Mattel had gone through a traumatic leadership and financial period. All this had taken its toll dramatically on the dolls. By 1973, *Barbie* dolls were available that, in my opinion, were not much better than the dime store dolls competing with them.

Some toy companies saw this as opportunity knocking. Here was the first real chance in almost 15 years to "dethrone" *Barbie*, the queen of teen fashion dolls. The women's movement was in full swing. Athletes like Billy Jean King were telling women that the best way to compete in a man's world was aggressively. Suddenly the movement for some went to extreme. Masculine looking women, with chopped hairstyes, seemed to overtake the

278. LJN's *Brooke Shields, The World's Most Glamourous Teenage Doll*. A stunningly realistic portrait doll, this challenger sold quite well in 1982 and 1983.

glamourous ones. Some women began to question why they were spending hours on makeup and hair. Was it to please themselves, or men, which were being viewed as oppressive by the mid 1970s.

In 1974, Kenner issued *Dusty*, a robust, athletic girl doll that was a sports figure. Her size was 12in (30cm), and she could not fit in *Barbie* clothes, not that she would have wanted to! *Dusty* and black girlfriend, *Skye*, for some mothers gave their daughters a chance at something more than a beauty parlour life. Little girls were involved in lawsuits to be allowed to play on boys' sports teams. Like other minorities, the pendulum of their desires would swing too far, then settle back again. For now, some feminists saw *Dusty* as the perfect rebellion against the glamour image. The public, however, saw things differently. Not

279. The 1980s has opened up the world of rock star fashion dolls. Creata has introduced *Lace*®, an exciting rock band that features wild fashions. The dolls are unnamed, adding to play value.

Lace® is a registered trademark of Creata.

to be used as pawns, little girls who not yet faced sex discrimination seemed not as interested in proving a point as did their mothers. Mattel quickly got their problems straightened out, and Kenner learned that *Dusty* was not the answer to the long run that *Barbie* had enjoyed. The mistake they made, in my opinion, is that *Barbie* has been kept current, BUT feminine. Like "Charlie's Angels," *Barbie* did not sacrifice glamour for adventure. Little girls seemed to agree, for *Dusty* "hit

the dust" after a brief run. Kenner was not ready to give up, however.

As previously discussed, the late 1970s saw the birth of the club culture. Dressing up, disco dancing and going out were the new American pastimes. Glamour was back more than ever, and Kenner again entered the fashion doll race with one of the finest products ever produced.

In 1978, *Darci* was introduced. A top fashion model AND cover girl, *Darci* was a high quality, 12in (30cm) doll that had setable nylon hair that was fully-rooted and very stylable, with a wardrobe of up-to-the-minute fashions. *Darci*, as a blonde, brunette or redhead, lived the "Charlie's Angels" type of life that was so popular. The doll was simply stunning. A beautiful store display captured the

Darci® and *Dusty*® are registered trademarks of Kenner.

attention of the buying public. *Darci* was the embodiment of all that American women stood for. Beautiful, sophisticated, independent, talented and athletic, *Darci* had a strong, but feminine personality. A friend, *Erica*, was added to the line, as well as *Dana*, *Darci's* counterpart in black. Lucky is the collector who has put away these fine dolls, for they are truly lovely and of the finest quality. Each outfit came with a small cover of a magazine such as *New Woman, Bride's Magazine* or *Disco Scene* that featured *Darci* on the cover.

Added to the line was a van which *Darci* drove herself to her location shots, a modeling studio that had working lights, and a Disco, which she designed herself, and owned and operated. *Darci* was a positive role model for any young girl who saw herself as wanting to get involved with life. No mention of a boyfriend or future plans for children were mentioned, but the implication was that if *Darci* wanted it, she could have it, and not have to sacrifice to get it. Perhaps the supporters of *Dusty* could say that *Darci* was also damaging to personalities by making "superwoman" a goal, but most would say that it is by striving for perfection and falling short that we become the best we can be.

Darci was, in my opinion, the perfect fashion doll. If this is true, then why was she discontinued after just three years? I believe by 1980, most households had several ages of children. Toys were handed down, or at least shared, and *Darci* did not fit into *Barbie*-size clothing. This necessitated the expense of an entire new wardrobe for *Darci*. After years of furnishing children with cases of *Barbie*-size garments, many families simply rebelled against this added play expense. Many, myself included, observed this in

280. Madonna, the music icon of the 1980s, is the inspiration for today's fashion dolls. Like a complete circle, Madonna's Marilyn Monroe image parallels the early teen fashion dolls! *Movie Star News photograph.*

person when shopping for *Darci*. Many children were told that if the doll were brought home, "She would have nothing to wear." Of course, what Kenner had hoped for was just that, except the response would be to PURCHASE the new wardrobe. One must remember that the economic situation in the early 1980s did not often include such an outlay. We collectors, eager to sacrifice grocery money, new clothing or vacations to have the dolls we want, must remember that we are buying these items to love and cherish and not turn over to a child to destroy. Many saw the investment as not worthy of the cost. Adding to the demise of *Darci* was that television advertising was strong at first, but seemed weak later on. By 1980, television was the best source of advertising for a doll; the decision of

Dusty® *Darci*®, *Erica*® and *Dana*® are registered trademarks of Kenner.

171

281. Hasbro's *Jem®* and boyfriend, *Rio®*. The story of *Jem®* is a complicated one. Highly developed and well thought out, *Jem's®* fashions and music tell a wonderful story.

Jem® and *Rio®* are registered trademarks of Hasbro, Inc.

what toys a child played with were mostly decided by the child and NOT the parent as had been the case in the 1950s.

Clearly the 1980s brought changes to teen fashion dolls. Celebrity dolls (dolls which were made to look like the person intended), became a focal point of collecting. Effanbee's *W. C. Fields* was the first doll in years that was actually sculpted after the character intended instead of created by wigs and clothing. LJN figured if celebrity dolls were selling so well, a celebrity FASHION doll would surely be a hit. Using model Brooke Shields, they issued at Toy Fair, 1982, a *Barbie*-size doll with her likeness. The doll was beautifully made, facially, but the quality of the body, in my opinion, and the neck structure, were not quite right. The slogan of the manufacturer at Toy Fair that year was, "Go For Brooke," urging retailers to "go for broke" and order heavily. The doll,

according to the company, was highly successful, but must have been over-produced, as discount stores carried the doll half price from 1985 on. It still can be found for under $5.00 with some prudent scouting. Again, if the doll interests you, grab it now, as it will be an outstanding collectible of the future. Always a mirror of current trends, fashion dolls became for many children the way to play in the world of outrageous "punk" fashions that they themselves could not risk ridicule by wearing in their own neighborhoods. Many an adult collector of 1980s fashion dolls would come up with the same motive, I am sure. Rock stars like Madonna, Sheena Easton and others manner of "stage" dressing could only be worn every day in some place like New York City. Those children from other towns had to act out this type of dress through doll play.

W. C. Fields® is a registered trademark of W. C. Fields Productions, Inc.

Mattel again had a winner with *Barbie and The Rockers*. With so many rock stars denouncing drugs and alcohol, parents seemed more confident to let their children be creative and carefree within limits. *Barbie* as a rock star showed that you could dress outrageously and still be "wholesome." It was like a whole new market had opened up for dolls. Suddenly, just like in the early 1960s, there was room for other dolls. Children, both girls and boys, (the stigma of dolls was easing somewhat for boys) enjoyed playing "rock star band" with this type of doll in shared play.

One company, Creata, issued their own rock star band, *Lace*, in 1986. Their feeling was that just like Whitney Houston is ONE popular singer, there are lots more just as popular. While *Barbie and The Rockers* was one top band, *Lace* could be another! *Lace* featured unnamed girls with outrageous clothing. A black doll, which was especially lovely, featured a 1960s hairstyle in the tradition of the girl groups of the time like the Chiffons. *Lace* is another doll that if the collector is interested in, would do well to purchase right away. One never knows when a rock star, or a rock star doll is going to fade from public view!

Another chapter to our fashion doll anthology was a really serious contender. Hasbro, long known for doing things "right" came up with *Jem*, one of the most fantastic dolls of the 1980s.

Jem had her own story, her own band, her own orphanage, AND her own competition, *The Misfits* built right into her world. With boyfriend *Rio*, and a popular animated series, *JEM* was the first serious competition *Barbie* had had since *Darci* in the late 1970s.

Lace® is a registered trademark of Creata.

Jem®, *The Misfits*® and *Rio*® are registered trademarks of Hasbro, Inc.

Darci® is a registered trademark of Kenner.

Unfortunately, *JEM* was withdrawn from the market after a two year trial run. In fact, catalogs and the entire *Jem* line had been designed for 1988. A decision was made to withdraw the doll and go with a "safer" fashion doll, *Barbie* sized, named *Maxie*. The reason *Jem* failed is that like those before her, her larger size meant that clothing already at home for other dolls could not be used on her. Also, her personality of a rock star, singer was one dimensional, and Hasbro executives felt that it had a limited audience. This is all most unfortunate for the collector, for *JEM* was tailor made for the fashion doll collector. Hasbro's new doll, *Maxie* is basically the concept that *Barbie* was originally founded on...the story of a beautiful teen-age girl and her life. Hasbro has yet to hook a personality on *Maxie*, but if she survives, she will gradually develop into some sort of role as is being planned with a television series, "Maxie's World" which will establish character for the doll.

Hasbro tried to make *Maxie*, "safe," by having her be just like any girl next door. But "safe" meant boring to doll collectors who, for the most part, saw nothing collectible in *Maxie*. The doll was a dismal failure and was quickly discontinued. In all fairness, *Maxie* and especially her boyfriend *Rob*, were well made. The gift sets and clothing were of superior quality. Hasbro announced it would not compete in the near future with *Barbie*.

Not many companies have attempted to dethrone *Barbie* recently, but there have been some very interesting dolls on the market.

Matchbox, well known for its toy car line, introduced *The Real Model Collection*. The collection focused on likenesses of Beverly Johnson, a black model who was very successful in the late 1970s and 1980s. The set also featured Christie Brinkley, whose face is very visible; and the then 44-year-old beauty, Cheryl Tiegs. The dolls were of excellent quality,

but facial resemblances were not apparent. It was doubtful that many children had heard of the three models, with Christie Brinkley being the exception.

Kenner once again decided to enter the race and introduced *The Miss America Collection* at the 1991 Toy Fair. It featured very high quality dolls, costumes, and packaging. The dolls came in two versions, an evening gown for competition and a talent outfit. There was a black contestant, *Tonya*, to help inspire black children. The dolls looked, in my opinion, a bit "cartoonish," and there has been a legal dispute over the dolls between Kenner and Mattel.

Mattel has indeed gone out in the 1990s to make sure they capture all markets. A marketing study done around 1989, identified the top fourteen cities with high concentrations of black residents. Using this knowledge, and listening to consumer complaints and suggestions, Mattel issued their *Shani* line of ethnically correct, Afro-American dolls in 1991. The line was available in three skin tones and with ethnic features. The dolls were stunning and the clothing was brilliantly designed. Other dolls in the line included *Asha* and *Nichelle*.

In another move, Mattel made a fantastic doll likeness of rap singer *M C Hammer*. Available in stage clothing with a "boom box" (large radio, for the uninitiated), the doll is perhaps the best celebrity likeness Mattel has ever done.

Noting the success of Tyco's *The Little Mermaid* dolls from the Disney animated feature, Mattel also made Disney licensed dolls of *Cinderella* and *Prince Charming* that coincided with the re-release of the Disney classic. Having had success with these two dolls, and all their accessories, (including "masks" of the evil stepmother and the fairy godmother), dolls representing *The Beast* and *Belle* were rushed to the market in late 1991 to capitalize on the release of Disney's fantastic animated film, *Beauty and the Beast*. All of these dolls used *Barbie* and *Ken* bodies, so clothing could be interchanged. It is certainly a fascinating time for the fashion doll collector!

Epilogue

Almost daily, collectors of fashion dolls are reporting new and unusual discoveries in old warehouses, or fascinating current items gathered in travels to other countries.

Because the leader of the pack of fashion dolls is *Barbie*, and because she is the ONLY teen fashion doll to survive a tumultuous three decades, the heart of this book must go to the illustration of the hundreds of dolls and fashions produced by Mattel over the years.

As a teen fashion doll fan, my goal has been to acquaint the collector of this genre of doll with ALL the choices available. The collector of *Tammy* is missing a lot by not knowing *Barbie*. The person who limits their knowledge to just one area loses by not at least viewing the other selection of dolls available. Obviously, space and money are always a consideration in any collection, but this book has attempted to acquaint the novice, and tease the advanced collector with a panorama of teen fashion dolls.

Barbie and other fashion dolls satisfy in a human being the need for continuity in one's life...a feeling that the glorious past and the brillant future are united. Since fashion doll collectors in general, and *Barbie* doll collectors in particular, seem to be upwardly mobile individuals with a strong sense of self worth, it seems safe to say that the teen fashion doll collectors' world is indeed a golden one.

It is difficult to say entirely what has made *Barbie* and these other dolls the inspiration to so many. Psychologists have written many a thesis on the personality of *Barbie*, in particular, and the contribution she has made to our culture.

We, as collectors, can only be thankful that *Barbie*, *Tammy*, *Tressy* and a host of others were there to share our realities and enhance our memories. We hope there will always be *Barbie* and other fashion dolls for a child and a collector to love together.

282. The ultimate *Barbie* collectible for 1991 was The Wedding Party Gift Set. It featured six dolls, including the new *Kelley* and *Todd* dolls.

The Barbie® Family & Friends Tree*

* All of the names present in this chart and the following price guide are protected names. The legal protections were left off for the readability of this chart and the price guide charts.

			Celebrity Licensed Friends	International Barbies
	Skipper — Friends —	Ricky		Royal Barbie
		Skooter	Twiggy	Parisian Barbie
		Fluff	Truly Scrumptious	Italian Barbie
		Tiff	Julia	Oriental Barbie
		Ginger	Miss America	Scottish Barbie
		Scott	Donny Osmond	India Barbie
		Courtney	Marie Osmond	Eskimo Barbie
		Kevin	Jimmy Osmond	Spanish Barbie
	Francie — Friends—	Casey	Kitty O'Neill	Swedish Barbie
			Kate Jackson	Irish Barbie
	Tutti		Cheryl Ladd	Swiss Barbie
Relatives	& — Friends		Debbie Boone	Japanese Barbie
	Todd		Kristy McNichol	Peruvian Barbie
	Kelley (Wedding Gift Set)		Buffy & Mrs. Beasley	Greek Barbie
	Jazzie — Friends—	Chris	M C Hammer	German Barbie
	Todd (Wedding Gift Set)	Dude		Icelandic Barbie
		Stacie	Foreign Friends	Canadian Barbie
		Chelsea	Carla	Korean Barbie
			Valerie	Mexican Barbie
	Ken — Friends —	Allan	Chantel Goya	Russian Barbie
		Brad	Flora	Nigerian Barbie
		Curtis	Ellie	Brazilian Barbie
		Todd (Groom)	Living Eli (Japan)	Malaysian Barbie
		Derek	Tulie Chan (Japan)	Czechoslovakian Barbie
BARBIE®		Steven	Skip Chan (Japan	Australian Barbie
			Noel (Japan)	Native American Barbie
	Midge		Stephanie (Japan)	Reissues of:
	Christie		Sophie (Japan)	Parisian Barbie
	Stacey		Wayne Gretsky	Eskimo Barbie
	P.J.		Bob (Rio version of Ken)	Scottish Barbie
	Jamie		Kotbie ┐	Spanish Barbie
	Steffie		Danbie ├ Korea	English Barbie
	Kelley			Italian Barbie
	Cara		Lia ┐	
	Tracy (Bride)		Diva │	
Friends	Miko		Vicky ├ Brazil	Outer Space Friends
	Dana		Bobby ┘	Sun Spell
	Dee Dee			Moon Mystic
	Diva		Marina ┐	
	Whitney		Laura ├ Europe	
	Teresa			
	Bopsy		Monica ├ India	
	Becky			
	Belinda			
	Kayla			
	Deyon			
	Nia			
	Nikki			
	Kira			
	Tara Lynn			

	Honey		Acquaintances
	Midnight		Lori 'N Rori
	Dallas		Angie 'N Tangie
	Pups of Beauty		Nan 'N Fran
	Dixie	Pet Animals w/O.F.'s or Sets	Heart Family
	Prince	Put Ons and Pets — black Poodle	(Mom, Dad, Girl, Boy,
	Tahiti	Put Ons and Pets — Afghan	Baby and cousins)
	Fluff	Put Ons and Pets— white cat	Heart Family's
	Prancer	Scottie — Skipper's Dog Show	Grandparents
	Dog 'N Duds	Dog — Tutti's "Me and My Dog"	Trueheart
	Dancer	Jamie's grey Poodle	(Heart Family Dog)
	Beauty	Jamie's white Poodle	Asha
	Turquoise	Skipper's Terrier	Shani
Pets	Sun Runner	Kevin's Dalmation	Nichelle
	Star Stepper		Jamal
	Snow Ball	Babies	Cinderella
	Zizzi Zebra	Barbie Baby-Sits Baby	Prince Charming
	Ginger Giraffe	Sears Baby-Sits Baby	Belle
	Blinking Beauty	Baby Sitter Skipper	The Beast
	Sachi	Black Baby Sitter Skipper	Sleeping Beauty
	Honey	Baby Sitter Courtney	The Princess Jasmine
	Wags	Heart Family Cousins	Alladin
	Tiffy	Mertwins	
	Chelsie (Skipper)		
	Butterfly (Stacie)		
	Western Star		

1992, A Most Exciting Barbie* Year

The excitement was electric at Toy Fair, 1992. It would prove to be a most exciting year in *Barbie* history.

With much fanfare and stunned surprise, *My Size Barbie* was unveiled. Standing at almost three feet tall, she was an imposing sight! Offered on a limited trial basis to certain areas, the child could share the clothing the doll was wearing! (Adult collectors could only dream or squeeze!)

Teen Talk Barbie was the ultimate in mechanical dolls. Each doll could be combined with fashion colors, hair shades, and eye colors, to be unique. With black versions, the quantities of different dolls available were seemingly endless.

One phrase the doll ably uttered was "Math class is tough"; the press seized the moment to decry the remark as sexist. Since I am sure that countless numbers of little boys, myself included, have stated the same fact, the point was lost on all but collectors who had to purchase a doll to determine what she spoke!

The Classique Collection was one of the most gorgeous lines every unveiled by Mattel. Beginning with the outstanding, legendary designer Carol Spencer, *Benefit Ball Barbie* was a knockout with real rooted eyelashes and red hair. Her long gown, one of Carol's signature creations, made the doll the talk of New York.

Bob Mackie was featured with two new additions to the Timeless Creations line. *Neptune's Fantasy* and *Empress Bride* versions of *Barbie* were both worthy of museum collections.

Mass market dolls also included *Totally Hair Barbie* and friends, which sported the longest hair ever on a *Barbie* doll. At the end of the year, Mattel announced that it was the best selling *Barbie* of all time! In a bold marketing move, and a successful attempt to keep *Barbie* current, the doll would be discontinued at the end of the year, just like automobile manufacturers did in past decades. *Totally Hair Ken* enthralled collectors with his rooted pompadour hairstyle and new face mold. Equally intriguing was the older *Ken* face also used on some dolls.

One of my personal 1992 favorites was *Rappin' Rockin' Barbie* and friends. Dressed

283. Above: From Fox Television Network teen drama "Beverly Hills, 90210" comes Mattel's line of fashion dolls, featuring likenesses of characters (from left to right), Brandon (Jason Priestley), Brenda (Shannen Doherty) and Dylan (Luke Perry). In addition, Mattel will produce dolls based on characters Kelly (Jennie Garth) and Donna (Tori Spelling). *Photograph courtesy Mattel, Inc.*

284. Below: *Sleeping Beauty* awaits the kiss from *Prince Phillip* in Disney Classics Collection by Mattel. *Photograph courtesy Mattel, Inc.*

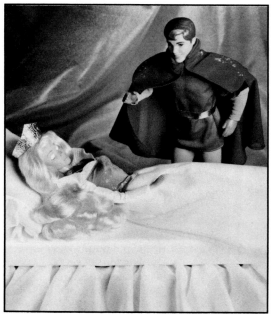

up to the minute in hip-hop style, they each came with a working boom box that featured a particular beat. When played together, it was first class style just like a rock video soundtrack!

Just when you thought every trend for the year had been covered, *Rollerblade Barbie* and friends skated across the Mattel showroom. Based on the famous brand name *Rollerblade* single line skates, a dazzling "spark" was created when *Barbie* and the gang were skating.

The lead glamour dolls were *Sparkle Eyes Barbie and Ken.* With the use of rhinestone chips, *Barbie's* eyes glimmered and shined when the lights hit them.

Mattel once again issued a ponderous list of store specials for not only familiar names such as Toys R Us, and Target, but the membership wholesale warehouses as well. It would prove a difficult year of keeping up for the collector. Mattel stated it was the best financial year ever for *Barbie*, despite the "recession economy." The new collector was ever dazzled as the prestigious store, F.A.O. Schwarz, opened "Barbie Boutique," featuring the latest in *Barbie* merchandise for all ages.

The year 1992 would also see the cementing of the Mattel and Disney empires with the *Disney Classics* series continuing with heart stopping characters such as *Belle* and *The Beast* among others. While not part of the *Barbie* line, fashion doll collectors grab up these high quality dolls. Especially noteworthy were the gift sets featuring even more movie costumes from famous Disney animated features.

My first glimpses of the mystical *Jasmine* and *Alladin* from the fall 1992 Disney movie *Alladin* were at Toy Fair, when Mattel previewed to the press its movie classics line-up.

Collectors would agree that 1992 was perhaps the most successful attempt by Mattel to meet their needs with quality dolls and theme selection.

285. *Sparkle Eyes*™ *Barbie*® and *Sparkle Surprise*™ *Ken*®. *Photograph courtesy Mattel, Inc.*

286. **World of Barbie collectibles, the** *Empress Bride*™ *Barbie*® **in a Bob Mackie original.** *Photograph courtesy Mattel, Inc.*

1993, Collector's Influence Barbie®

For 1993 it was evident that the fashion doll collector who specialized in *Barbie* was a powerful force in the decision making process at Mattel. Timeless Creations, the collectors division of Mattel, Inc., had unveiled yet another line of *Classique* dolls and fashions. This time the mega talented Janet Goldblatt would have TWO special dolls that would be unique. *City Style Barbie* was dressed for a day of shopping in a major metropolitan area, and *Opening Night Barbie* would be the ultimate in moderately priced collectors dolls. Featuring real rooted eyelashes and brunette shoulder length hair, the doll was an instant hit. The costume was so well received that Janet would wear an exact replica while attending "You've Come Along Way Barbie," the 1993 Barbie Doll Collectors Convention held in Baltimore, Maryland. This event was hosted by The Busy Barbie Doll Collectors Club of Maryland and chaired by Mark Ouelette.

The Great Eras collection featured two outstanding dolls. The first, *Flapper Barbie*, was dressed in classical roaring twenties style, and featured rooted eyelashes and short, bobbed hair.

The second entry was entitled *Gibson Girl Barbie* and was a light brownette doll with rooted eyelashes. The packaging was superb.

One of the attractions to the collector, and children alike, is *Barbie's* way of mirroring what is popular in our culture.

Troll Barbie came dressed in troll printed pants and carried a real troll doll with hair that could be removed and used by the owner. Trolls are so popular today that this *Barbie* will always be remembered as a trend setter.

The *Western Stampin'* series of dolls featured *Barbie, Ken* and new friend *Tara Lynn* as country western dancers. Once again, the dolls are themed just like the current fad of line dancing to country music. *Tara Lynn*, especially dazzling with her raven black hair, pouty red lips, and red outfit, was a favorite among Toy Fair attendees.

For those who collect the porcelain dolls, there were two new offerings. It was *Barbie's* friend *Midge's* 30th anniversary,

287. The Great Eras™ Collection, *Gibson Girl Barbie®*. *Photograph courtesy of Mattel, Inc.*

Glamour dolls are always a big hit and *Secret Hearts Barbie* and *Ken* were certainly no exception. *Ken* looks astonishing like movie star Tom Cruise, much to the delight of many.

Earring Magic Barbie, in two hair colors, and friends *Midge* and *Ken* would cause quite a stir. The press picked up on *Ken's* earring and frosted hair and quoted statistics about how popular the doll was with Gay men. Like the "Math class is tough" tirade from 1992, it was much ado about nothing. But, the publicity is always exciting to the collector!

and *Midge* in porcelain as a red head was dressed in a recreation of *Senior Prom* with a "borrowed" white fur stole from *Barbie*. The other doll is a stunning brunette bubble cut *Barbie* in *Red Flair* with *Silken Flame* underneath.

The *Dolls of the World Collection* had three stunning new editions. *Native American Barbie* was a runaway hit, and with the popularity of the films *Dances with Wolves* and *Last of the Mohicans*, she fits right in! *Australian Barbie* and the newly reissued, but totally different, *Italian Barbie* rounded out the series.

Bob Mackie fans are dazzled with the introduction of *Harlequin Ball Barbie*, dressed for a masquerade ball and accented with Mackie perfume. This highly collectible and popular line is always a winner!

Barbie was once again serving our armed forces with an *Army Barbie* and *Ken*. Called *Stars* and *Stripes*, it represents our 101st Airborne division. Once again the *Ken* head mold with regulation hair cut was featured.

288. *1920's Flapper™ Barbie®* from the Great Eras Collection. *Photograph courtesy of Mattel, Inc.*

A personal favorite was *Paint N' Dazzle Barbie*. Not only did she come as a blonde, brunette, and red head, but she sported clothing and a car that could be customized with included paints and notions.

Angel Lights Barbie will sit on many a tree top this year! Enclosed in her gown are white lights that make her the perfect tree topper. And *Twinkle Lights Barbie* has a sparkling fiber optic bodice that makes the word colorful merely a cliche!

Also delightful to collectors was *Fountain Mermaid Barbie* that actually shoots a waterfall from the top of her crown! *Skipper*, dressed as a mermaid, was ready for water play and babysitting the *Mertwins*, two adorable babies.

The year 1993 will also be remembered as a year that many collectors broke a promise. After so many store specials and limited editions in 1992, many collectors, myself included, said that this year they were going to be "choosy." Nice work if you can find it! The 1993 specials from EVERY STORE were incredible! *Police Officer Barbie*, and *Spots N' Dots Barbie*, to *Barbie Learns to Read*, to Home Shoppers *Winter Princess Barbie*...they all have one thing in common! They are gorgeous, limited, and destined to rise in value, especially now that so many new collectors are entering the market. One surprise doll was *Little Debbie Snacks Cake Barbie*, which was a mail in premium and had brunette hair. Even Kool-Aid brand soft drinks had a great street style fashion *Barbie* doll mail in premium that featured very unusual artwork on the packaging. Like most other collectors, I juggled non existent space and bought duplicates of dolls I thought would rise rapidly in value! It was a tremendous year.

289. *Troll Barbie*® **doll has four plush hair tufts—lavender, pink, yellow and blue.** *Photograph courtesy of Mattel, Inc.*

290. *Twinkle Lights Barbie*® is a sparkling rainbow in an iridescent dress trimmed with fiber optics that light up and change color. *Photograph courtesy of Mattel, Inc.*

1994, Barbie's® 35th Anniversary!

It looks like 1994 is going to be another out of sight year! It is *Barbie's* 35th Anniversary, and the *Nostalgic Barbie* line will be around again, as it was in 1989. This time, Mattel has announced plans for a reissue number one *Barbie* in vinyl, reasonably priced and available as a blonde or brunette, AND in a gift set with replica editions of the first discontinued outfits from 1959, *Gay Parisienne, Roman Holiday Separates*, and *Easter Parade*. The big question is, how will this affect the value of the older dolls and outfits! I think it will increase the awareness of the vintage items and will help the entire market in general.

Also planned is a continuation of the *Great Eras Collection* with the introduction of *Egyptian Barbie* and *Southern Belle Barbie*. The *International Collection* or *Dolls of the World Collection* will see another version of *Native American Barbie*, and a new African country, as well as *China Barbie* added to this already outstanding collection.

Yes, it is a doll's life. If you lived at my house, it would be your life also, for *Barbie* is indeed a cup that runneth over! As long as Mattel is putting out such tempting treats, AND the vintage and special dolls continue to rise so in value, I guess that we collectors will keep collecting. It is indeed a challenge for us long time collectors.

Fashion doll collecting is FUN! Why not get started today?

Teen Fashion Doll Price Guide

by A. Glenn Mandeville

In this 4th, revised edition of *Doll Fashion Anthology*, it is evident how much the doll world has changed since the third edition in 1991! New trends are emerging that are both exciting, yet confusing. Let me try to summarize what is happening in the fashion doll world.

• There has been a shift in the *Barbie®* collecting world from an emphasis on the vintage dolls, to much attention paid to newer dolls, especially store specials and limited editions. Those who collect vintage dolls and clothing (often defined as dolls and fashions from 1959-1972) are collecting one of three ways. An ever growing number of collectors are seeking out the never removed from box fashions. Because this supply is limited, prices are rising for the rarer fashions and some popular mod era clothing as well. The second type of collector is buying excellent condition dolls and fashions out of box to display on dolls. Still a third type of collector is piecing outfits together, often keeping elaborate notebooks of pieces and parts needed to complement what they already have.

• *Barbie®* as a fashion mannequin for designers, other than Mattel, is a growing trend. Using Mattel dolls as a basis for their designs, this talented group of individuals is rerooting hair, repainting faces, and sometimes recreating entirely new characters out of existing dolls and their own materials. Prices for these dolls rival vintage dolls in some cases!

• The restoration of badly played with dolls is now a booming business. This trend seems encouraging to those on limited budgets or to those who are artistically inclined and love a challenge. The results, when rendered by a professional, are often beyond what a mass marketed doll once looked like. The consensus seems to be for restoring a doll that would otherwise be discarded.

• Ideal *Tammy*™, and American Character *Tressy®* items, never removed from box or even mint, complete, are almost impossible to locate. For scme reason the first editions of these dolls and fashions are somewhat easier to find than later 1960s editions. In my opinion, if fashion doll collectors desired some of these outfits and gift sets, they would be almost impossible to locate. Expect to pay very high prices for NRFB *Tammy* and *Tressy* items. The value guide is based on what the average collector would be willing to pay and not an isolated high price on a particular item; however, to the right collector, just having the opportunity to buy would set a higher price than listed.

• The fashion doll market is one of the strongest areas in collecting. Conventions, magazines, and new collectors arriving daily, feed an ever increasing market for exciting new dolls and superior vintage items. It would be safe to say that values will continue to rise indefinitely as the increasing publicity attracts new collectors.

• The popularity of fashion doll collecting is based upon the several levels of collecting that exist within the same market and the fact that the level of one's collecting seems to matter little in social gatherings of fashion doll collectors. Unlike other types of dolls, a "new" collector can shop beside a seasoned veteran at the local toy store! This phenomenon is perhaps the leading reason why the fashion doll collector network is so large and appealing. After all, doll collecting is FUN and the friendships lasting!

INSTRUCTIONS:
   PLEASE READ CAREFULLY!

The prices given are for "Never Removed From Box Dolls," or "Mint in Box Dolls" where applicable. Allow slightly more for a pristine box with no markings, outfits that still have the seal with the outfit name, and ultra mint dolls and packaging. SUBTRACT ONE-HALF of this price for any doll or outfit, no matter how mint, that is missing the box. SUBTRACT ANOTHER 25% if the item is played with.

Tammy™

Points to Remember

Points to remember when pricing Tammy dolls and accessories.

Tammy items do surface often mint in box. The doll was overproduced, and much old store stock still survives, almost 30 years later!

Out of box outfits are actually harder to find than mint in box outfits! There is not much price difference between a mint in box outfit and one complete out of box. The prices given can be used both ways.

There is, however, still a 50% difference between an out of box doll and one in the box. *Mom* is worth $55 in the box and $29.50 out.

Look for prices on these dolls to rise sharply within the next five years as fashion doll collectors assimilate the rest of the old store stock into their collections.

Tammy, basic doll in box in blue
playsuit, complete with stand and
booklet . . . .$ 50 up
    Black **Tammy** $300
Pos 'n Tammy . . . .$ 95
Other editions . . . .$ 50
Glamour Misty . . . .$ 75 up
Pos 'N Misty . . . .$ 75 up
Mom, Dad, Ted, Pepper . . . .$ 45
Dodi . . . .$ 55
Pete (hard to find) . . . .$ 95
Tammy's Ensemble Outfits
    Beau and Arrow . . . .$ 55
    Checkmate . . . .$ 45
    Cheerleader Outfit . . . .$ 45
    Cutie Co-Ed . . . .$ 55
    Dream Boat . . . .$ 55
    Figure 8 . . . .$ 55
    Fun in the Sun . . . .$ 55
    Fur 'N formal . . . .$ 95
    Knit Knack . . . .$ 50
    Model Miss . . . .$ 95
    Picnic Party . . . .$ 60
    Pizza Party . . . .$ 55
    Puddle Jumper . . . .$ 45
    Purl One . . . .$ 35
    Ring-a-Ding . . . .$ 35

    School Daze . . . .$ 35
    Skate Date . . . .$ 45
    Sleepytime . . . .$ 35
    Snow Bunny . . . .$ 75
    Sorority Sweetheart . . . .$ 75
    Travel Along . . . .$ 35
    Underwear Outfit . . . .$ 25
    Walking Her Pet . . . .$ 75
1964-1965 Couture Outfits . . . .$ 75 up
Mom Outfits:
    Evening in Paris . . . .$ 75
    Hidden Glamor . . . .$ 75
    Lazy Days . . . .$ 50
    Lounging Luxury . . . .$ 50
    Nighty Nite . . . .$ 50
    Shopping Topping . . . .$ 45
Pepper Outfits:
    After School Fun . . . .$ 30
    Bed Time . . . .$ 25
    Class-Room Caper . . . .$ 35
    Frosty Frolics . . . .$ 35
    Nylon Undies . . . .$ 35
    Party Time . . . .$ 40
Ted and Dad Outfits:
    Clothes on Card (sweaters,
    slacks, jackets, trousers,
    shorts, pajamas, etc.): . . . .$ 30 up

Tressy®

Points to remember when pricing *Tressy* dolls and accessories.

Tressy items are the hardest to find mint in box. One almost never sees the outfits out of box complete, either. American Character did not overproduce their outfits.

Gift sets with a doll and makeup or hair accessory are worth double the price of the single doll.

Tressy dolls, fashions and accessories are destined to be very valuable in the future. If an item seems a bit high today, buy it anyway as it will be even higher tomorrow!

Basic Tressy mint in box . . . .$ 95
Black versions $300
Tressy with posable knees . . . .$ 75
Mary Make-Up . . . .$ 75 up
Cricket . . . .$ 45
Hi-Fashion Cosmetic Kit . . . .$ 35
Tressy's Apartment . . . .$150 up
Tressy's Beauty Shoppe $150
Tressy's Hair Coloring . . . .$ 25 set
Fashions...
Tressy
   Black Magic . . . .$ 75
   Blue Ribbon Winner . . . .$ 95
   Bon Voyage . . . .$ 95
   Campus Casual . . . .$ 50
   Check Mates . . . .$ 75
   Executive Sweet . . . .$ 40
   Fifth Avenue . . . .$ 75

Good News . . . .$ 50
Hootenanny . . . .$ 50
Kitchen Cutie . . . .$ 75
Lazy Days . . . .$ 40
Miss American Character . . . .$150 up
Miss Suburbia . . . .$ 35
Pink Champagne . . . .$ 75
Sailing Party . . . .$ 55
Sugar 'N Spice . . . .$ 25
Window Shopping . . . .$ 55
Simple dresses on cards . . . .$ 20 up
Cricket Fashions
   Hootenanny . . . .$ 35
   School Days . . . .$ 25
   Ship Ahoy . . . .$ 20
   Sugar 'N Spice . . . .$ 25
   Windy Weather . . . .$ 20

Judy Littlechap®

The Littlechap Family
(Mint in box)
    Dr. John Littlechap ....$ 50 up
    Judy Littlechap ....$ 50 up
    Libby Littlechap ....$ 50 up
    Lisa Littlechap ....$ 50 up
Dr. John's Outfits:
    Dr. John's Medical Outfit ......$ 55
    All Weather Coat ....$ 25
    Business Suit ....$ 35
    Golf Outfit ....$ 25
    Pajamas ....$ 20
    Tuxedo ....$ 55
Judy's Outfits:
    Bathing Ensemble ....$ 25
    Dance Dress ....$ 30
    Football Outfit ....$ 45
    Nightshirt ....$ 20
    Pajamas ....$ 20
    Party Dress ....$ 25
    Red Chesterfield Coat ....$ 45

    Sportswear Outfit ....$ 20
    Three-Piece Suit ....$ 45
Libby's Outfits:
    Levis and Sweatshirt ....$ 20
    Lingerie ....$ 15
    Pajamas ....$ 15
    Plaid Reefer Coat ....$ 20
    Three-Piece Blazer Outfit ......$ 20
    Ya Ya Dress ....$ 20
Lisa's Outfits:
    Basic Black Dress ....$ 25
    Formal Evening Ensemble .....$ 75
    Fur-Trimmed Suede Coat ......$ 45
    Lingerie ....$ 20
    Peignoir and Nightgown Ensemble $ 25
    Three-Piece Chanel Suit ....$ 45
    White Two-Piece Dress ....$ 45
Playsettings:
    Dr. John's Office ....$100 up
    Littlechap Family Room ....$100 up
    Littlechap Master Bedroom ......$100 up

Et Al

Points to remember when pricing other teen fashion dolls.

Your eye for quality is the best guide of all. There are dozens of teen fashion dolls that were poor quality. Yesterday's junk is still tomorrow's junk! Just because something is 30 years old does not make it a fine collectible.

Do not put off till tomorrow what you can buy today. Generic fashion dolls have a very short shelf life. Like cottage cheese, they will be discarded when expired. Make your purchase NOW and avoid disappointment.

Most fashion dolls are really a bargain. This might not always be the case as more collectors enter the field and supplies decrease. The LJN *Brooke Shields* doll may be on sale in your area now, but in another year or two, be impossible to find!

Brenda Starr dolls...
Basic doll in box . . . . $200 up
with extra wig . . . . $250 up
Dressed dolls in box.
Beach Outfit . . . . $200 up
Shirt waist dress . . . . $200 up
Flower print dress $150
Bride $350
Formals $350
extra boxed outfits
(more for formals) . . . . $ 75 each

Yolanda (same doll as
Brenda Starr)
Turquoise satin formal $350
Bride $350
Tulle formal $350

Dusty by Kenner
Dusty doll, basic in box . . . . . . $ 55
Skye doll, basic in box . . . . $ 55
Action set, doll with sports
accessory . . . . $ 65
Fashions . . . . $ 25 each

Darci by Kenner
Basic Darci . . . . $ 45
Department Store Special Darci
with extra dress . . . . $ 75
Dana . . . . $ 50
Erica (very hard to find) $150
Darci's Modeling Studio . . . . . . $ 75
Darci's Disco . . . . $ 75

Darci Fashions:
All That Glitters . . . . $ 35
Autumn Days . . . . $ 30

Bermuda Longs . . . . $ 30
Blue Angels . . . . $ 30
Bronco Blue . . . . $ 30
Copper Overalls . . . . $ 30
Dream Girl . . . . $ 30
Fancy Dancer . . . . $ 30
Fancy Pants . . . . $ 30
Fire Cracker . . . . $ 30
Garden Gal . . . . $ 30
Green Light . . . . $ 30
In the Pink . . . . $ 30
Jean Scene . . . . $ 30
Mellow Yellow . . . . $ 30
Party Perfect . . . . $ 30
Red, White and You . . . . $ 30
Sheer Delight . . . . $ 30
Simply Smashing . . . . $ 30
Singin' In the Rain . . . . $ 30
Slim Jim Girl . . . . $ 30

Darci Lifestyle Fashions:
Disco Gold . . . . $ 40
Fur Fantasy . . . . $ 40
Garden Party . . . . $ 40
Hi Roller . . . . $ 40
Lovely Lavender . . . . $ 40
Plum Perfect . . . . $ 40
Running Free . . . . $ 40
Sensational Senorita . . . . $ 40
Suit Yourself . . . . $ 40

Perfect Pose Fashions:
Blue Lightning . . . . $ 45
Pink On Point . . . . $ 45
Wedding Belle . . . . $ 45

1994 *Barbie*® Price Guide

NAME OF DOLL	NRFB* VALUE
ALLAN	
Bendable Legs	$ 250
Dressed Boxed Doll	$ 800 up
Straight Legs	$ 95
ANGIE 'N TANGIE	$ 250
BABS	$ 150
BARBIE	
Angel Face	$ 30
Astronaut	$ 50
Baggies	$ 55-95
Ballerina	$ 30
Beautiful Bride	$ 200
(real lashes)	$ 250
Beauty Secrets	$ 40
1965 Bendable Legs	$ 700
1966 Bendable Legs	$1200
Bendable Legs (side-part hair)	$3500
Black	$ 45
Bubble Cut	$ 275
Busy	$ 200
Busy Talking	$ 275
Color Magic	$1400
Crystal	$ 30
Day-to-Night	$ 25
Dream Date	$ 30
Dream Glow	$ 20
Dreamtime	$ 15
Dressed Boxed Doll	$ 300 up
Pink Silhouette Dressed Boxed Doll	$ 800 up
Wedding Day Set (value depends upon whether doll and stand are #1, #2, or #3 doll)	$1500 up
Eskimo	$ 150
Fashion Jeans	$ 20
Fashion Photo	$ 65
Fashion Queen	$ 500
Feelin' Groovy	$ 140
Free Moving	$ 65
Funtime	$ 15
Gift Giving	$ 15
German	$ 75
Golden Dream	$ 40
Gold Medal	$ 90
Gold Medal Set	$ 95
Gold Medal Skater	$ 95
Gold Medal Skier	$ 75
Great Shape	$ 15
Growing Pretty Hair (pink, 1971)	$ 295
(blue, 1972)	$ 295
Hair Fair	$ 85
Hair Happenin's	$ 800
Happy Birthday (white)	$ 25
(pink)	$ 25
Hawaiian	$ 40
Hispanic	$ 60
Horse Lovin'	$ 30
India	$ 125
Italian	$ 195
Japanese	$ 100
Jewel Secrets	$ 20
Kissing	$ 45
Kissing (with bangs)	$ 60
Live Action	$ 150
Live Action On Stage	$ 175
Living	$ 175
Loving You	$ 60
Magic Curl	$ 30
Magic Moves	$ 25
Malibu (1971)	$ 30
Miss Barbie	$1500
My First	$ 25
Newport	$ 125

* **Never Removed From Box**

Number #1 Ponytail	
Blonde	$3400
Brunette	$3800
Number #2 Ponytail	
Blonde	$3200
Brunette	$3500
Number #3 Ponytail	$ 800
Number #4 Ponytail	$ 500
Oriental	$ 150
Parisian	$ 125
Peaches 'n Cream	$ 30
Pink & Pretty	$ 35
Plus Three	$ 50
Ponytail (1962-1965)	$ 400
Pretty Changes	$ 35
Quick Curl	$ 60
Quick Curl Deluxe	$ 75
Rocker (1986)	$ 30
Rocker (1987)	$ 30
Roller Skating	$ 50
Royal	$ 250
Scottish	$ 150
Sears Celebration	$ 60
Standard	
(1967-1970)	$ 300
(1970-1972)	$ 325
Spanish	$ 115
Sun Gold Malibu	$ 18
Sun Lovin'	$ 25
Sunsational	$ 25
Sun Valley	$ 150
Super Hair	$ 20
Supersize	
Beautiful Bride	$ 165
Super Hair	$ 150
Super Star	$ 150
Super Star Fashion	
Change-Abouts	$ 90
In The Spotlight	$ 70
Promotional	$ 85
Swedish	$ 95
Sweet 16	
Promotional	$ 75
Regular	$ 65
Swirl Ponytail	$ 425
Talking	$ 275
Talking Spanish	$ 300
Tropical	$ 15
Twirly Curls	$ 25
Twist 'N Turn	$ 300
Walk Lively	$ 195
Ward's Anniversary	$ 600
Western	$ 20
Wig Wardrobe	$ 195
BARBIE BABY-SITS SETS	
1963-1965	$ 250
1974-1976	$ 55
BOONE, DEBBY	$ 45
BRAD	
Bendable Legs	$ 125
Talking	$ 135

BUFFY & MRS. BEASLEY	$ 150
CARA	
Ballerina	$ 25
Free Moving	$ 25
Quick Curl	$ 25
Quick Curl Deluxe	$ 35
CASEY	
Baggie	$ 40
Twist 'N Turn	$ 250
CHRIS	
1967-1968	$ 150
1974-1976 (Re-issue)	
(European)	$ 75
CHRISTIE	
Beauty Secrets	$ 25
Fashion Photo	$ 55
Golden Dream	$ 35
Kissing	$ 45
Live Action	$ 140
Malibu (1973)	$ 35
Pink & Pretty	$ 55
Sun Lovin'	$ 35
Sunsational	$ 25
Supersize	$ 95
Super Star	$ 75
Talking	$ 175
Twist 'N Turn	$ 195
CURTIS	
Free Moving	$ 45
DANA	
Rocker (1986)	$ 25
Rocker (1987)	$ 25
DEE-DEE	
Rocker (1986)	$ 25
Rocker (1987)	$ 25
DEREK	
Rocker (1986)	$ 25
Rocker (1987)	$ 25
DIVA	
Rocker (1986)	$ 25
Rocker (1987)	$ 25
FLUFF	$ 135
FRANCIE	
Baggie	$ 100
Bendable Legs	$ 200
Black	$ 950
Busy	$ 275
Growin' Pretty Hair	$ 150
Hair Happenin's	$ 295
Malibu (1971)	$ 45
Quick Curl	$ 65
Straight Legs	$ 150
Twist 'N Turn	$ 325
(no bangs)	$ 850
GINGER	
Growing Up	$ 55
JACKSON, KATE	$ 25
JAMIE	
Walking	$ 175
JULIA	
Talking	$ 125

Twist 'N Turn
(2-piece suit) ....$ 125
(1-piece suit) ....$ 75
KELLEY
Quick Curl ....$ 75
Yellowstone ....$ 175
KEN
All Star ....$ 25
Baggies ....$ 25
Bendable Legs
(old face) ....$ 250
(new face) ....$ 95
Busy ....$ 150
Busy Talking ....$ 125
Crystal ....$ 25
Day-to-Night ....$ 25
Dream Date ....$ 25
Dream Glow ....$ 20
Dressed Boxed Doll ....$ 300
Fashion Jeans ....$ 30
Flocked Hair ....$ 150
Free Moving ....$ 40
Gold Metal Skier ....$ 80
Great Shape ....$ 20
Hawaiian ....$ 30
Horse Lovin' ....$ 25
Jewel Secrets ....$ 20
Live Action ....$ 95
Live Action On Stage ....$ 135
Malibu (1971) ....$ 20
Mod Hair ....$ 150
Now Look ....$ 55
Painted Hair/Straight Legs .....$ 115
Rocker ....$ 20
Roller Skating ....$ 30
Sport 'N Shave ....$ 30
Sun Lovin' ....$ 20
Sun Gold Malibu ....$ 20
Sunsational ....$ 20
Sun Valley ....$ 80
Super Star ....$ 75
Talking ....$ 125
Talking Spanish ....$ 125
Tropical ....$ 15
Walk Lively ....$ 75
Ward's Dressed ....$ 115
Western ....$ 25
LADD, CHERYL ....$ 30
LORI 'N RORI ....$ 175
McNICHOL, KRISTY ....$ 25
MIDGE
Bendable Legs ....$ 550
Dressed Box Doll ....$ 800 up
Straight Legs ....$ 150
Wig Wardrobe ....$ 200
MIKO
Tropical ....$ 15
MISS AMERICA
Quick Curl Blonde ....$ 35
Quick Curl Brunette ....$ 45
Walk Lively ....$ 150

MOON MYSTIC ....$ 75
NAN 'N FRAN ....$ 125
O'NEILL, KITTY ....$ 25
OSMONDS
Donny ....$ 45
Marie ....$ 45
Donny & Marie together ......$ 55
Jimmy ....$ 65
P.J.
Baggies ....$ 45
Fashion Photo ....$ 45
Free Moving ....$ 45
Gold Medal Gymnast ....$ 75
Live Action ....$ 95
Live Action On Stage ....$ 115
Malibu (1972) ....$ 30
Quick Curl ....$ 45
Quick Curl Deluxe ....$ 65
Sun Gold Malibu ....$ 20
Sun Lovin' ....$ 20
Sunsational ....$ 20
Sweet Roses ....$ 35
Talking ....$ 125
Twist 'N Turn ....$ 225
RICKY ....$ 95
SCOTT
Superteen ....$ 55
SKIPPER
Baggie Pose 'N Play ....$ 60
Bendable Legs ....$ 225
Dressed Boxed Doll ....$ 300 up
Great Shape ....$ 20
Growing Up ....$ 65
Horse Lovin' ....$ 25
Jewel Secrets ....$ 20
Living ....$ 55
Malibu (1971) ....$ 25
Quick Curl ....$ 65
Quick Curl Deluxe ....$ 80
Straight Legs ....$ 150
Sun Gold Malibu ....$ 20
Superteen ....$ 45
Re-issue (1970) ....$ 125
Tropical ....$ 15
Twist 'N Turn ....$ 175
Western ....$ 25
SKOOTER
Bendable Legs ....$ 290
Straight Legs ....$ 125
STACEY
Talking ....$ 275
Twist 'N Turn
(side ponytail) ....$ 275
(short turned up hair) ....$ 295
STEFFIE
Busy ....$ 175
Busy Talking ....$ 250
Walk Lively ....$ 150
SUN SPELL ....$ 75
TIFF
Pose 'N Play ....$ 250

TODD
- 1967-1970 ....$ 150
- 1974 re-issue (European) ....$ 95
- Sunday Treat Set with Tutti .....$ 450

TODD (Groom) ....$ 25

TRACY (Bride) ....$ 25

TRULY SCRUMPTIOUS
- Straight Legs ....$ 350
- Talking ....$ 375

TUTTI
- Cookin' Goodies ....$ 350
- Me and My Dog ....$ 400
- Melody In Pink ....$ 350
- Night Night Sleep Tight ......$ 250
- 1967-1971 ....$ 125
- 1974 re-issue (European) ......$ 75
- Re-issue Playsettings (European) ....$ 95
- Sundae Treat Set with Todd ....$ 450
- Swing-A-Ling ....$ 350
- Walkin' My Dolly ....$ 275

TWIGGY ....$ 225

WHITNEY
- Jewel Secrets ....$ 40

FOREIGN DOLLS OF INTEREST

BARBIE
- Equestrienne ....$ 75
- Fabulous Fur ....$ 35
- Golden Nights (Disco) ....$ 35
- Jeans ....$ 35
- Music Lovin' ....$ 35
- Playtime ....$ 55
- Picture Pretty ....$ 55
- Rio ....$ 75 up
- Safari ....$ 55 up
- Sea Lovin' ....$ 35
- Snow Princess ....$ 250
- w/Skooter Gift Set ....$ 250
- Sporting ....$ 95
- P.B. (Ma-Ba) ....$ 175

BOB
- (Rio version of Ken) ....$ 150 up

CARLA ....$ 75

CHAN, TULIE ....$ 150 up

ELLIE ....$ 75

FLORA ....$ 75

GOYA, CHANTAL ....$ 150

GRETSKY, WAYNE ....$ 55

KEN
- Golden Nights (35) ....$ 35
- Jeans ....$ 35
- Music Lovin' ....$ 35
- Safari ....$ 55 up
- Sea Lovin' ....$ 35

SKIPPER
- Golden Nights (Disco) ....$ 35
- Jeans ....$ 35
- Music Lovin' ....$ 35
- Safari ....$ 55 up
- Sea Lovin' ....$ 35

TAKARA (most notable)
- Excelina ....$ 125
- Kansai ....$ 195
- Mink ....$ 900
- Nakano ....$ 250
- Romantic ....$ 250

VALERIE
- Hollywood ....$ 250
- Tahitiana ....$ 250

POPULAR MISCELLANEOUS ITEMS — MINT CONDITION
- Airplane ....$ 800
- Bed, Barbie's Suzy Goose ....$ 55
- Bed, Skipper's Suzy Goose ......$ 55
- Car, Barbie's first ....$ 75
- Cases ....$ 10 up
- College ....$ 350
- Deluxe House, Barbie & Skipper's ....$ 200
- Dream House, Barbie's first ......$ 75
- Dream Kitchen and Dinette, Barbie's ....$ 500
- Fashion Shop ....$ 300
- Furniture, Go-Together (each set) ..$ 55
- Hot Rod Car, Ken's ....$ 95
- Little Theatre ....$ 500
- Piano, Barbie's Suzy Goose ......$ 350
- Posing Stand, first ....$ 800 up
- Skipper Dream Room ....$ 500
- Vanity & Bench, Barbie's Suzy Goose ....$ 55
- Vanity & Bench, Skipper's Suzy Goose ....$ 55

POPULAR GIFT SETS — NRFB VALUE
- Party Set $1800
- Mix 'N Match (Ponytail) $1500
- (Bubble-Cut) $1000
- Trousseau Set $3000
- Fashion Queen Barbie & Her Friends ....$ 700
- Fashion Queen Barbie & Ken Trousseau $1800
- Barbie & Ken (tennis o/f) $1500
- Barbie & Ken Little Theatre $2800
- Barbie, Ken & Midge on Parade $2000
- Barbie, Ken & Midge Pep Rally ....$ 700
- Barbie's Sparkling Pink ....$ 950
- Barbie's Round the Clock ....$ 950
- Barbie's Wedding Party $2800
- Barbie Hostess $2500
- Midge's Ensemble $1200
- Midge Mix N Match ....$3000 up
- Skipper Party Time ....$ 400
- Skipper On Wheels ....$ 400

POPULAR SEARS GIFT SETS
- Barbie "Movie Groovy" ....$ 350
- Barbie "Perfectly Plaid" ....$ 350
- Barbie Travel In Style Set ....$ 500
- Casey Goes Casual ....$ 700

Color Magic Barbie ....$1500 up	Orange Blossom ....$ 100
Francie and her Swingin' Separates .$ 500 up	Party Date ....$ 150
Francie "Rise 'N Shine" ....$ 500 up	Peachy Fleecy Coat ....$ 95
Malibu Ken "Surf's Up" ....$ 350	Picnic Set ....$ 250
Live Action P.J.	Plantation Belle ....$ 300
"Fashion 'N Motion" ....$ 350	Red Flair ....$ 125
Living Fluff "Sunshine Special" ....$ 250	Registered Nurse ....$ 150
Stacey "Nite Lightning" ....$ 850	Resort Set ....$ 125
Stacey "Stripes Are Happening" ....$ 850	Roman Holiday Separates
Talking Julia "Simply Wow" ......$ 500 up	(completely NRFB) ....$3000 up
Walking Jamie "Furry Friends" ....$ 500	Senior Prom ....$ 175
Walking Jamie "Strollin In Style" ..$ 500	Sheath Sensation ....$ 100
STORE DISPLAY SETS ....$1000 up	Silken Flame ....$ 125
CLOTHING **NRFB VALUE**	Singing in the Shower ....$ 75
(listed by period)	Ski Queen ....$ 125
BARBIE: Early Period	Solo in the Spotlight ....$ 275
1959-1963	Sophisticated Lady ....$ 250
After 5 ....$ 100	Sorority Meeting ....$ 175
Apple Print Sheath ....$ 125	Stormy Weather ....$ 75
American Airlines Stewardess .....$ 175	Suburban Shopper ....$ 200
Ballerina ....$ 150	Sweater Girl ....$ 125
Barbie Accessories ....$ 300	Sweet Dreams ....$ 175
Barbie Baby-Sits	Swingin' Easy ....$ 125
(apron) ....$ 250	Tennis Anyone ....$ 50
(layette) ....$ 300	Theatre Date ....$ 125
Barbie-Q Outfit ....$ 125	Wedding Day Set ....$ 350
Bride's Dream ....$ 175	Winter Holiday ....$ 175
Busy Gal ....$ 300	**BARBIE LITTLE THEATRE**
Busy Morning ....$ 225	**COSTUMES 1964**
Candy Striper Volunteer (1964) ....$ 350	Barbie Arabian Nights ....$ 275
Career Girl ....$ 250	Cinderella ....$ 295
Cheerleader (1964) ....$ 175	Guinevere ....$ 225
Commuter Set ....$ 800	Red Riding Hood and
Cotton Casual ....$ 125	the Wolf ....$ 400
Cruise Stripe Dress ....$ 125	**BARBIE TRAVEL OUTFITS 1964**
Dinner at Eight ....$ 200	Barbie in Hawaii ....$ 200
Drum Majorette ....$ 150	Barbie in Holland ....$ 200
Easter Parade ....$2500 up	Barbie in Japan ....$ 375
Enchanted Evening ....$ 225	Barbie in Mexico ....$ 200
Evening Splendour ....$ 175	Barbie in Switzerland ....$ 200
Fancy Free ....$ 95	**BARBIE:**
Fashion Undergarments ....$ 125	**Couture Period 1964-1966**
Floral Petticoat ....$ 125	Aboard Ship ....$ 250
Friday Nite Date ....$ 200	Barbie Learns to Cook ....$ 300
Garden Party ....$ 95	Barbie Skin Diver ....$ 100
Gay Parisienne ....$2000 up	Beautiful Bride (1967) $1300
Golden Elegance ....$ 200	Beau Time ....$ 225
Golden Girl ....$ 195	Benefit Performance ....$ 850
Graduation ....$ 50	Black Magic Ensemble ....$ 250
Icebreaker ....$ 125	Brunch Time ....$ 250
It's Cold Outside (1964) ....$ 125	Campus Sweetheart ....$ 800
Knitting Pretty	Caribbean Cruise ....$ 150
(blue) ....$ 350	Club Meeting ....$ 250
(pink) ....$ 300	Country Club Dance ....$ 300
Let's Dance ....$ 125	Country Fair ....$ 125
Masquerade ....$ 150	Crisp 'N Cool ....$ 140
Mood For Music ....$ 125	Dancing Doll ....$ 350
Movie Date ....$ 100	Debutante Ball ....$ 850
Nighty-Negligee ....$ 125	Disc Date ....$ 225
Open Road ....$ 250	Dog 'N Duds ....$ 250

Dreamland . . . .$ 125
Evening Enchantment (1967) . . .$ 475
Evening Gala . . . .$ 275
Fabulous Fashion . . . .$ 475
Fashion Editor . . . .$ 300
Fashion Luncheon . . . .$ 950
Floating Gardens (1967) . . . .$ 400
Formal Occasion (1967) . . . .$ 450
Fraternity Dance . . . .$ 425
Fun at the Fair . . . .$ 230
Fun 'N Games . . . .$ 230
Garden Tea Party . . . .$ 125
Garden Wedding . . . .$ 370
Golden Evening . . . .$ 185
Golden Glory . . . .$ 295
Gold 'N Glamour . . . .$ 800
Here Comes The Bride . . . .$ 950
Holiday Dance . . . .$ 395
International Fair . . . .$ 375
Invitation to Tea . . . .$ 350
Junior Designer . . . .$ 250
Junior Prom . . . .$ 425
Knit Hit . . . .$ 125
Knit Separates . . . .$ 125
London Tour . . . .$ 295
Lunch Date . . . .$ 90
Lunch on the Terrace . . . .$ 250
Lunchtime . . . .$ 200
Magnificence . . . .$ 450
Matinee Fashion . . . .$ 350
Midnight Blue . . . .$ 500
Miss Astronaut . . . .$ 750
Modern Art . . . .$ 325
Music Center Matinee . . . .$ 500
On the Avenue . . . .$ 400
Outdoor Art Show . . . .$ 375
Outdoor Life . . . .$ 200
Pajama Party . . . .$ 85
Pan American Airways
  Stewardess . . . .$2000 up
Poodle Parade . . . .$ 550
Pretty as a Picture . . . .$ 350
Reception Line . . . .$ 385
Riding in the Park . . . .$ 400
Satin 'N Rose . . . .$ 250
Saturday Matinee . . . .$ 700
Shimmering Magic $1500
Skater's Waltz . . . .$ 285
Sleeping Pretty . . . .$ 200
Sleepytime Gal . . . .$ 225
Slumber Party . . . .$ 200
Sorority Tea . . . .$ 175
Student Teacher . . . .$ 275
Sunday Visit . . . .$ 350
Underfashions . . . .$ 350
Vacation Time . . . .$ 200
White Magic . . . .$ 185

BARBIE: The Mod Period 1967-1971

These outfits are rapidly rising in value. Because of the overwhelming number of outfits produced during this period, fashions are broken up as follows:

NRFB

A. Street dresses that are unelaborate with few accessories such as Knit Hit, Midi Magic, Snap-Dash, etc. . . . .$ 75 up
B. Fancy dress sets with lots of accessories that are Mod looking like Zokko!, All That Jazz, Sparkle Squares and Julia and Twiggy fashions also . . . .$ 125 up
C. Ball gowns and bridal outfits such as Romantic Ruffles, Silver Serenade, Winter Wedding, Let's Have a Ball, etc. . . . .$ 175 up

BARBIE: The Passive Seventies Period 1972-1976

The 1970s fashions are of much poorer quality. The ones that are collectible are those which correctly show the fashions of the period. Look for outfits like peasant dresses, granny gowns and bell-bottoms!

NRFB

A. Fashions on blister cards . . . .$ 35
B. Get-Ups 'N Go fashions . . . .$ 35
C. Boxed, fancy, highly accessorized fashions . . . .$ 45

BARBIE: The Disco Daze Period 1977-1979

Disco outfits tell the story of dressing up. The fancy, glittery gowns with boas are the most desirable.

NRFB

A. Simple Dresses . . . .$ 25
B. Designer Originals . . . .$ 25
C. Super Star Fashions . . . .$ 35

BARBIE: The Energetic Eighties Period

Few of the 1980s fashions are yet high priced. Use this opportunity to keep your collection current! Most are only worth original prices. Special outfits that make a fashion statement are priced at double the original price.

NRFB

A. Collector Series . . . .$ 45
B. Oscar de la Renta Collector Series $ 45

Collectible Barbie Price Guide

This price guide centers on the *Barbie* department store specials and dolls issued through Timeless Creations, the collector's division of Mattel, Inc. Most of the dolls from Timeless Creations have come packed in shipping cartons, with styrofoam inserts, etcetera. To see the product, one had to open the box, if for no other reason, to make sure that all the parts were contained within. Because of this, prices refer to mint dolls, with *all* accessories that came with that doll. The value is not lessened, in my opinion, because someone opened the box to check the contents, or displayed the doll in the case provided.

Porcelain Barbie
- 1986 *Blue Rhapsody Barbie* . . . . $ 750
- 1987 *Enchanted 1960 Barbie* . . $ 350
- 1988 *Benefit Performance 1967 Barbie* . . . . $ 450
- 1989 *Wedding Party 1959 Barbie* . . . . $ 525
- 1990 *Solo in The Spotlight 1961 Barbie* . . . . $ 185
- 1990 *Sophisticated Lady Barbie* . . . . $ 185
- 1991 *Gay Parisienne 1959 Barbie* . . . . $ 180
- 1991 *Thirtieth Anniversary Ken, 1961* . . . . $ 200
- 1991 *Gay Parisienne 1959 Barbie* (Red or Blonde Hair) . . $ 450
- 1992 *Plantation Belle Barbie* . . $ 210
- 1992 *Plantation Belle Barbie* (Walt Disney World) . . . . $ 450
- 1992 *Crystal Rhapsody Barbie* . $ 175
- 1993 *30th Anniversary Midge* . . $ 200
- 1993 *Silken Flame Barbie* . . . . $ 200
- 1993 *Crystal Rhapsody Barbie* (Disneyland) (Brunette) . . . . . $ 350
- 1993 *Royal Splendor Barbie* (direct purchase) . . . . $ 189
- 1993 *Gold Sensation Barbie* (direct purchase) . . . . $ 179

Happy Holiday Barbie
- 1988 . . . . $ 400
- 1989 . . . . $ 110
- 1990 (white) . . . . $ 95
- 1990 (black) . . . . $ 75
- 1991 (white) . . . . $ 75
- 1991 (black) . . . . $ 55
- 1992 (white) . . . . $ 65
- 1992 (black) . . . . $ 50
- 1993 (white) . . . . $ 38
- 1993 (black) . . . . $ 38

Special Editions
- 1988 *Mardi Gras Barbie* . . . . . . $ 85
- 1989 *Pink Jubilee Barbie* $1500
- 1989 *UNICEF Barbie* (four nationalities) . . . . $ 35 each
- 1989 *Army Barbie* . . . . $ 30

- 1990 *Air Force Barbie* . . . . $ 35
- 1990 *Summit Barbie* (four races) . . . . $ 35 each
- 1990 *Wedding Fantasy Barbie* (white and black versions) . . . . $ 30 each
- 1991 *Dream Bride Barbie* . . . . . $ 40
- 1991 *Navy Barbie* (black and white) . . . . $ 20
- 1991 *Swan Lake Barbie* . . . . $ 125
- 1992 *Marine Corps Barbie* (black or white) . . . . $ 22
- 1992 *Marine Corps Ken* . . . . . . $ 22
- 1992 *Marine Corps Barbie and Ken Gift Set* . . . . $ 45
- 1992 *My Size 3ft Barbie* . . . . . . $ 140
- 1992 *Nutcracker Barbie* . . . . . . $ 110
- 1993 *Army Barbie* (Desert Storm) (black and white) . . . . $ 22
- 1993 *Army Ken* (Desert Storm) . $ 22
- 1993 *Army Barbie and Ken Gift Set* (Desert Storm) . . . . . . $ 45
- 1993 *Romantic Bride* . . . . $ 35
- 1993 *Gibson Girl Barbie* . . . . . . $ 60
- 1993 *1920s Flapper Barbie* . . . . $ 60

F.A.O. Schwarz Exclusives
- 1989 *Golden Greetings Barbie* . $ 150
- 1990 *Winter Fantasy Barbie* . . . $ 150
- 1991 *Night Sensation Barbie* . . . $ 135
- 1992 *Madison Avenue Barbie* . . $ 95
- 1993 *Rockettes Barbie* . . . . $ 95

Bob Mackie Barbie Collection
- 1990 *Designer Gold Barbie* . . . . $ 175
- 1991 *Platinum Barbie* . . . . $ 135
- 1991 *Starlight Splendor Barbie* . $ 125
- 1992 *Empress Bride Barbie* . . . . $ 220
- 1992 *Neptune's Daughter Barbie* . . . . $ 150
- 1993 *Masquerade Ball Barbie* (Harlequin) . . . . $ 196

Designer Classics
- 1992 *Benefit Ball Barbie* (Carol Spencer) . . . . $ 60
- 1993 *Opening Night Barbie* (Janet Goldblatt) . . . . $ 60
- 1993 *City Style* (Janet Goldblatt) . . . . $ 60

Other Selected Store Specials

(Note: It is my opinion that not all store specials are collectible. The ones listed are those that have risen in value since issue, or should be purchased while available.)

1988 Selected Specials

Equestrienne Barbie
(Toys R Us) ....$ 45
Lilac and Lovely Barbie
(Sears) (black and white) .....$ 45
Tennis Barbie and Ken
(Toys R Us) ....$ 40
Sweet Dreams Barbie
(Toys R Us) ....$ 35

1989 Selected Specials

Dance Club Barbie with
recorder (Child World) ......$ 45
Party Lace Barbie (Hills) ......$ 25
Peach Pretty Barbie (K-Mart) ..$ 40
Evening Enchantment Barbie
(Sears) ....$ 45
Party Pink Barbie
(Winn-Dixie) ....$ 20
Gold 'N Glitter Barbie (Target) .$ 35
Lavender Look Barbie
(Wal-Mart) ....$ 25
Special Expressions Barbie
(Woolworth) (black and white) .$ 18
Denim Deluxe Barbie
(Toys R Us) ....$ 25
Pepsi Barbie Set (Toys R Us) ..$ 35
Pepsi Skipper Set (Toys R Us) ..$ 35
Sweet Treats Barbie
(Toys R Us) ....$ 35
Sweet Roses Barbie
(Toys R Us) ....$ 35

1990 Selected Specials

Disney Barbie (Child World)
(black and white) ....$ 35
Dance Magic Barbie and *Ken*
Gift Set ....$ 45
Evening Sparkle (Hills) ....$ 30
Dream Fantasy Barbie
(Wal-Mart) ....$ 25
Pink Sensation Barbie
(Winn-Dixie) ....$ 20
Special Expressions Barbie,
Second Edition (Woolworth) ..$ 15
Party Sensation Barbie
(wholesale clubs) ....$ 75
Western Fun Barbie and
Sun Runner Gift Set ....$ 55
Barbie Style (Applause) ....$ 35

1991 Selected Specials

Barbie Collector Doll
(Applause) ....$ 35
Cute 'N Cool (Target) ....$ 20
Golden Evening Barbie
(Target) ....$ 20
Ballroom Beauty Barbie
(Wal-Mart) ....$ 20

Sterling Wishes Barbie
(Speigel) ....$ 95
All American Barbie and
Star Stepper Gift Set
(wholesale clubs) ....$ 55
Jewel Jubilee Barbie
(Sam's Club) ....$ 35
Southern Beauty Barbie
(Winn-Dixie) ....$ 20
Moonlight & Roses Barbie
(Hills) ....$ 20
Party in Pink Barbie (Ames) ...$ 20
Blue Rhapsody Barbie
(Service Merchandise) ....$ 25
Sweet Romance Barbie
(Toys R Us) ....$ 25
School Fun Barbie (Toys R Us) .$ 25
Blossom Beauty Barbie
(Shopko/Venture) ....$ 25
Southern Belle Barbie (Sears) ..$ 35
Enchanted Evening Barbie
(J.C. Penney) ....$ 25
Beauty Pageant Skipper
(Toys R Us) ....$ 20
Barbie and Friends Gift Set
(Disney & Toys R Us) ....$ 55

1992 Selected Specials (editorial assistance courtesy of Mark Davidson)

Denim 'N Lace Barbie (Ames) .$ 30
Hot Looks Barbie (Ames) .....$ 25
Blue Elegance Barbie (Hills) ...$ 22
Evening Flame Barbie
(Home Shopping Club) ......$ 95
Evening Sensation Barbie
(J.C. Penney) ....$ 28
Pretty in Purple (black and
white) (K-Mart) ....$ 22
Something Extra Barbie
(Meijers) ....$ 20
Picnic Pretty Barbie (Osco) ....$ 20
Blossom Beautiful Barbie (Sears)$ 55
Satin Nights Barbie
(Service Merchandise) ....$ 35
Party Perfect Barbie
(Shopko/Ventures) ....$ 27
Regal Reflections Barbie
(Spiegel) ....$ 95
Party Premiere Barbie
(Supermarket Special) ....$ 20
Wild Style Barbie (Target) .....$ 20
Dazzlin' Date Barbie (Target) ..$ 25
Pretty in Plaid Barbie (Target) ..$ 25
Bathtime Fun Skipper (Target) .$ 18
Radiant in Red Barbie (black and
white) (Toys R Us) ....$ 35
Totally Hair Skipper
(Toys R Us) ....$ 20
Totally Hair Courtney
(Toys R Us) ....$ 20
Spring Parade Barbie Doll
(black and white) (Toys R Us) .$ 25

School Fun Barbie (black and
white) (Toys R Us) . . . .$ 20
Barbie for President Gift Set
(black and white) (Toys R Us) .$ 29
Cool 'N Sassy Barbie
(Toys R Us) . . . .$ 20
Anniversary Star Barbie
(Wal-Mart) . . . .$ 35
Royal Romance Barbie
(Price Club) . . . .$ 50
Very Violet Barbie (Pace) . . . .$ 40
Fantastica Barbie (Pace) . . . . . .$ 35
Peach Blossoms Barbie (Sams) .$ 25
Sweet Lavender Barbie (black
and white) (Woolworth) . . . . . .$ 23
Special Expressions Barbie
(black, white and Hispanic)
(Woolworth) . . . .$ 25
Cool Look Barbie (Toys R Us) .$ 20
Glamour Skipper (Toys R Us) . .$ 20
Dr. Barbie (Toys R Us) . . . .$ 20
Ski Fun Midge (Toys R Us) . . . .$ 25
(Some dolls may have been sold at other stores
than those listed.)
1993 Selected Specials
Country Looks Barbie (Ames) . .$ 25
Disney Fun Barbie (Disney) . . .$ 30
Golden Winter Barbie
(J.C. Penney) . . . .$ 25
Shopping Fun Barbie (Meijer) . .$ 22
Sparkling Splendor Barbie
(Service Merchandise) . . . .$ 35
Holiday Hostess Barbie
(Supermarket) . . . .$ 20
Spring Bouquet Barbie
(Supermarket) . . . .$ 20
Back to School Barbie
(Supermarket) . . . .$ 20
Golf Date Barbie (Target) . . . . .$ 20
Baseball Barbie (Target) . . . . . .$ 20
Malt Shop Barbie (Toys R Us) .$ 20
School Spirit Barbie (black and
white) (Toys R Us) . . . .$ 20

Police Officer Barbie (black and
white) (Toys R Us) . . . .$ 20
Moonlight Magic Barbie (black
and white) (Toys R Us) . . . . .$ 35
Spots 'N Dots Barbie
(Toys R Us) . . . .$ 22
Spots 'N Dots Teresa
(Toys R Us) . . . .$ 22
Love to Read Barbie
(Toys R Us) . . . .$ 25
*Western Barbie & Horse Gift
Set* (Toys R Us) . . . . .N/A
Radiant in Red (black and
white) (Toys R Us) . . . . .N/A
Super Star Barbie (black and
white) (Wal-Mart) . . . .$ 20
Winter Royal Barbie
(Wholesale Clubs) . . . .$ 20
Festiva Barbie (Sams) . . . .$ 30
Island Fun Gift Set
(Wholesale Clubs) . . . .$ 25
Hollywood Hair Gift Set
(Wholesale Clubs) . . . .$ 30
Western Stampin' Gift Set
(Wholesale Clubs) . . . . .N/A
Paint 'N Dazzle Gift Set
(Wholesale Clubs) . . . .$ 30
Secret Hearts Gift Set
(Wholesale Clubs) . . . . .N/A
Special Expressions (black,
white and Hispanic)
(Woolworth) . . . .$ 12
Royal Invitation (Spiegel) . . . . .$ 50
Little Debbie Barbie (Little
Debbie Snack Cakes) . . . .$ 35
Winter Princess Barbie
(Home Shoppers Club) . . . . . .$ 70

Note: The collector of these limited edition and
store special dolls would be advised to buy these
dolls while the supply is available.Though inex-
pensive now, it is certain that these dolls will rise
in value in future years because of the limited
number produced.

The values given within this book are intended as value guides rather than arbitrarily set prices. The
values quoted are as accurate as possible but in the case of errors, typographical, clerical or
otherwise, the author and publisher assume no liability nor responsibility for any loss incurred by
users of this book.

INDEX

(Bold numbers refer to illustration numbers.)